IMAGES
of America

GREAT SAND DUNES NATIONAL PARK

Ripples on the Dunes. Wind has created these rows of ripple marks, forming the illusion of a perfectly plowed field. Nat Dodge photographed this beautiful scene in October 1957, looking north across the dunes to Mount Herard. (GRSA-2617.)

On the Cover: Medano Creek, July 1987. Medano Creek was still flowing strong in July, much to the delight of visitors to Great Sand Dunes. The creek brings tons of sand down from the Sangre de Cristo Mountains to be deposited at the base of the dunefield and then it is blown back onto the dunes in the never-ceasing cycle of water, wind, and dune formation. (GRSA-5630-19.)

IMAGES
of America

GREAT SAND DUNES NATIONAL PARK

Mike Butler

ARCADIA
PUBLISHING

ISBN 978-0-7385-9694-5

Published by Arcadia Publishing
Charleston, South Carolina

Printed in the United States of America

Library of Congress Control Number: 2013932280

For all general information, please contact Arcadia Publishing:
Telephone 843-853-2070
Fax 843-853-0044
E-mail sales@arcadiapublishing.com
For customer service and orders:
Toll-Free 1-888-313-2665

Visit us on the Internet at www.arcadiapublishing.com

This book is dedicated to my wife, Mary Jane, and son Jason, and memories of our first visit to Great Sand Dunes in 1987.

Contents

ACKNOWLEDGMENTS

This book would not have been possible without the cooperation of the National Park Service staff at Great Sand Dunes National Park & Preserve. The majority of the photographs herein come from their archives. Special thanks to Patrick Myers, park ranger-interpretation, and Phyllis Pineda Bovin, biologist/museum curator, for generously sharing their time with me during the busy summer season. Thanks also go to Fred Bunch, chief of resource management. Another large group of photographs came from the Monte Vista Historical Society and their wonderful collection of San Luis Valley photographs by O.T. Davis. Thanks to Peg Schall for her assistance with that collection.

Family history is a very important part of this book, and I am grateful to Maria Causby for providing photographs and information about her ancestors, the Teofilo Trujillo family. Thanks also to Leona Wellington for her family photographs, details of the Wellington family tree, and recollections of her grandfather Frank Wellington.

Throughout the book, there are quotations from individuals and newspapers. Unless otherwise noted, quotations from individuals are from the book *Sand Stories*, while quotations from newspapers come from *Colorado Prospector* reprints of news articles.

While many people have helped with this project, any errors or omissions are completely the responsibility of the author.

Sources for the photographs in the book are annotated as follows: general collection of Great Sand Dunes National Park (GRSA), the museum collection of Great Sand Dunes National Park (GRSA-catalog number), the Monte Vista Historical Society (MVHS), photographs from individuals are noted by the names of their contributors, and all other photographs are from the author's collection.

INTRODUCTION

Located on the eastern edge of the San Luis Valley in south central Colorado, the Great Sand Dunes rise to a height of approximately 750 feet above the valley floor, which itself lies at an elevation of 7,500 feet above sea level. The dunes are the tallest in North America. The San Luis Valley is enclosed by the 14,000-foot peaks of the San Juan Range to the west and the 14,000-foot peaks of the Sangre de Cristo Range to the east. The Rio Grande River, flowing from northwest to southeast, is the only water flowing out of the valley. The San Luis Valley is the largest mountain valley in Colorado, approximately 100 miles long and 65 miles wide. Westerly winds blow sand particles (eroded from the volcanic rock of the San Juans) across the valley to gather against the Sangre de Cristos, where they come to rest in the huge dune formations. Water from Sangre de Cristo streams, flowing west, brings additional sand down from the mountains to be deposited in the dunes.

The area now included in the Great Sand Dunes National Park & Preserve has evolved over the years; it originated as American Indian hunting grounds, later encompassed large ranches and gold-mining claims, and then became a tourist attraction before achieving status as a national monument, and finally a national park. On November 22, 2000, Pres. Bill Clinton signed the Great Sand Dunes National Park and Preserve Act. The act expanded the size of the previous national monument from its original 46,034 acres to over 150,000 acres by adding 64,000 acres from the former Baca and Medano Ranches and transferring 42,000 acres from Rio Grande National Forest. Thus, the new Great Sand Dunes National Park & Preserve was created. The official declaration of the new national park had to wait until September 13, 2004, when the purchase of the former Baca Ranch was completed by the Nature Conservancy and the land transferred to the National Park Service.

Human occupation of the Great Sand Dunes area began approximately 11,000 years ago with the arrival of the Clovis people. These hunter-gatherers carved distinctive projectile points out of rock, which they used to hunt the ancient mammoths and bison in the area. Then, about 10,000 years ago, another (possibly related) hunter-gatherer group known as the Folsom people developed another type of distinctive projectile point for hunting. Fossilized bones of both mammoth and bison, carbon-dated to these time frames, have been found just south of Great Sand Dunes at the Zapata Ranch. For the millennia that followed, human occupation of the dunes area rose and fell cyclically, depending on the availability of water in the San Luis Valley.

When Spanish conquistadors from Mexico arrived in the San Luis Valley in 1599, they were greeted by various tribes of American Indians, including the Comanche, Apache, and Ute, who used the valley as hunting grounds for bison. Friendly relations between the Spaniards and American Indians did not last long. In one conflict with the Indians, a fatally injured Spanish priest glanced east to the mountains and saw them bathed in a red glow at sunset. Dying, he uttered, "*sangre de Cristo*," meaning "blood of Christ;" the name for the mountain range survives to this day. The Utes, capturing horses from the Spanish, became the dominant tribe in the valley, and more conflicts developed with Hispanic settlers from New Mexico who settled in the southern part of the valley beginning in 1851. Sporadic Ute raids continued in the valley until the Utes were finally subdued in the late 1880s.

The first recorded American citizens to see the Great Sand Dunes were Lt. Zebulon Pike and his men in January 1807. Pike was dispatched west by Pres. Thomas Jefferson to explore the great expanse of the lands obtained from France in the 1803 Louisiana Purchase. The boundary between the French land and Spanish Mexico was uncertain but was thought to be the Red River. Pike was, therefore, to find the Red River in order to establish the location of the United States' border with Mexico. Unfortunately, he began his mission into Colorado's mountains in the late fall of 1806. Starting along the Arkansas River west of Pueblo, he had already encountered heavy snow in the Wet Mountains. Pushing on—despite having to leave men behind with frozen feet—he crossed a mountain pass (either Medano Pass or Mosca Pass) over January 27 and 28, 1807. Looking westward down on the Great Sand Dunes, he wrote in his journal of seeing huge sand hills looking like a "sea in a storm." Proceeding down the mountains, past the dunes, Pike came upon the Rio Grande River, which he thought was probably the Red River. Realizing that he was now most likely on Spanish soil, he built a fort known as Pike's Stockade. The stockade was soon surrounded by Spanish troops, and Pike and his men were captured and sent to Mexico. They were later released on US soil.

Following Pike's expedition, fur trappers hunting beaver came to the Sangre de Cristo mountain passes in the 1830s. Mountain man Antoine Robidoux crossed Mosca Pass so many times that it was known as Robidoux's Pass until the 1850s, when the beaver were largely all trapped out. The United States officially gained all this territory from Mexico in a war that ended in 1848. Immediately after the defeat of the Mexicans, explorer John Charles Fremont, ignoring the lessons of Pike's wintertime expedition, started out in November 1848, seeking a railroad route west across the Sangre de Cristos. Facing terrible conditions, Fremont crossed Medano Pass, passing by the Great Sand Dunes on December 4, 1848. Snow in the San Luis Valley was very deep, and Fremont wandered around, losing 10 men and 120 mules, before being rescued by a search party from Taos on January 23, 1849. Capt. John Gunnison and his party had better luck searching for a railroad pass in August 1853, when they crossed Mosca Pass and saw "the most gigantic sandhills . . . shaped by the winds into beautiful and fanciful forms with waving outlines, for within certain limits this sand drifts about like snow." However, Mosca Pass was never used for a rail route, and Gunnison and seven of his men were killed by a Ute war party in Utah on October 26, 1853.

Hispanic and Anglo settlers in the San Luis Valley during the 1850s demanded protection from the US Army against the raiding Ute Indians. North of where Fort Garland is today, the Army established Fort Massachusetts in 1852. It was abandoned in 1858, when Fort Garland was built. When Indian raids finally decreased in the 1870s, large numbers of settlers came into the San Luis Valley with herds of cattle from Texas, establishing ranches right up to the edges of the Great Sand Dunes. Small ranches were soon gobbled up by larger ranches backed by investors and banks on the East Coast. Large ranches around the Great Sand Dunes included the Zapata Ranch to the south, Medano Ranch directly west, and Baca Ranch to the northwest. One of the first small ranchers, Teofilo Trujillo, established a ranch just west of Indian Spring in 1865. Trujillo built a beautiful adobe hacienda with stained-glass windows and the best of furnishings. He was constantly harassed by cattle rustlers and Ute Indians, and when he added sheep to his ranch, it was the last straw for the Anglo cattle ranchers. Built-up cultural tensions culminated with the burning down of Trujillo's home in 1902. The Trujillo family then dispersed to other areas in the San Luis Valley with more Hispanic settlers. Finally, in 1912, the combined Medano-Zapata Ranch came under the ownership of the G.W. Linger family, and tensions eased considerably.

Ranchers were followed by miners in the Great Sand Dunes area, and in the 1870s, virtually every mountain stream flowing west from the Sangre de Cristos was prospected for gold. John Duncan found gold on Milwaukee Hill, near Pole Creek, just north of the dunes. He built a cabin on Pole Creek and later began selling nearby lots to arriving miners. Despite the fact that he did not own the land, he sold 30 lots to settlers in 1892, and the town of Duncan was founded.

Duncan flourished with a hotel, grocery store, bakery, miner's supply store, saloon, and newspaper. All went for naught, however, when the true owner of the land (the owner of the Baca Grant) insisted that the miners leave the land in 1900. The owner made his point through harassment, even burning some of the miners' cabins. All the miners left Duncan, moving about a mile to the southeast, just outside the boundary of the Baca. Their new settlement was called, appropriately enough, Liberty. Today, the remains of Duncan and Liberty can be seen just outside the northeast boundary of Great Sand Dunes National Park.

By the late 1920s, the Great Sand Dunes were threatened on several fronts. Homesteaders inched ever closer to the dunes (the Wellington cabin is still standing in the national park, just a mile north of the Visitor Center). Gold miners were prospecting Medano Creek in what is now the national park, and sand from the dunes was being taken for use in cement and glass. Appalled, local residents called for protection of the dunes. Chambers of commerce from Pueblo to Del Norte recognized the tourist potential of the dunes, and all called for preservation. Local groups, such as the women's Philanthropic Educational Organization (PEO) chapter in Monte Vista and Alamosa, petitioned the Colorado Legislature to support preservation of the dunes in the US Congress. Finally, the National Park Service yielded to all the pressure and sent Yellowstone National Park superintendent Roger Toll to inspect the dunes area in 1931. Toll toured the dunes on February 13 and 14, 1931, and wrote a report recommending that "the land should be withdrawn from entry and established as a national monument." Pres. Herbert Hoover proclaimed the Great Sand Dunes National Monument on March 17, 1932.

In the 1980s, as scientists finally began to understand the effect of groundwater on the sustainability of the dunes, the geological integrity of Great Sand Dunes was threatened as the water company that owned the Baca Ranch proposed to export millions of gallons of groundwater by tunnel to the cities of Colorado's Front Range. It took a federal judge's order to stop this transfer of water, and the Nature Conservancy then actively began pursuing purchase of the Baca Ranch in order to preserve the underground water. The purchase of the combined Medano-Zapata Ranch in July 1999 protected the southern flank of the dunes, and with the completion of the purchase of the Baca Ranch in 2004, the northwest flank of the dunes also was protected. When the Nature Conservancy transferred a large portion of the Baca Ranch to the National Park Service, the Great Sand Dunes National Park & Preserve officially came into existence.

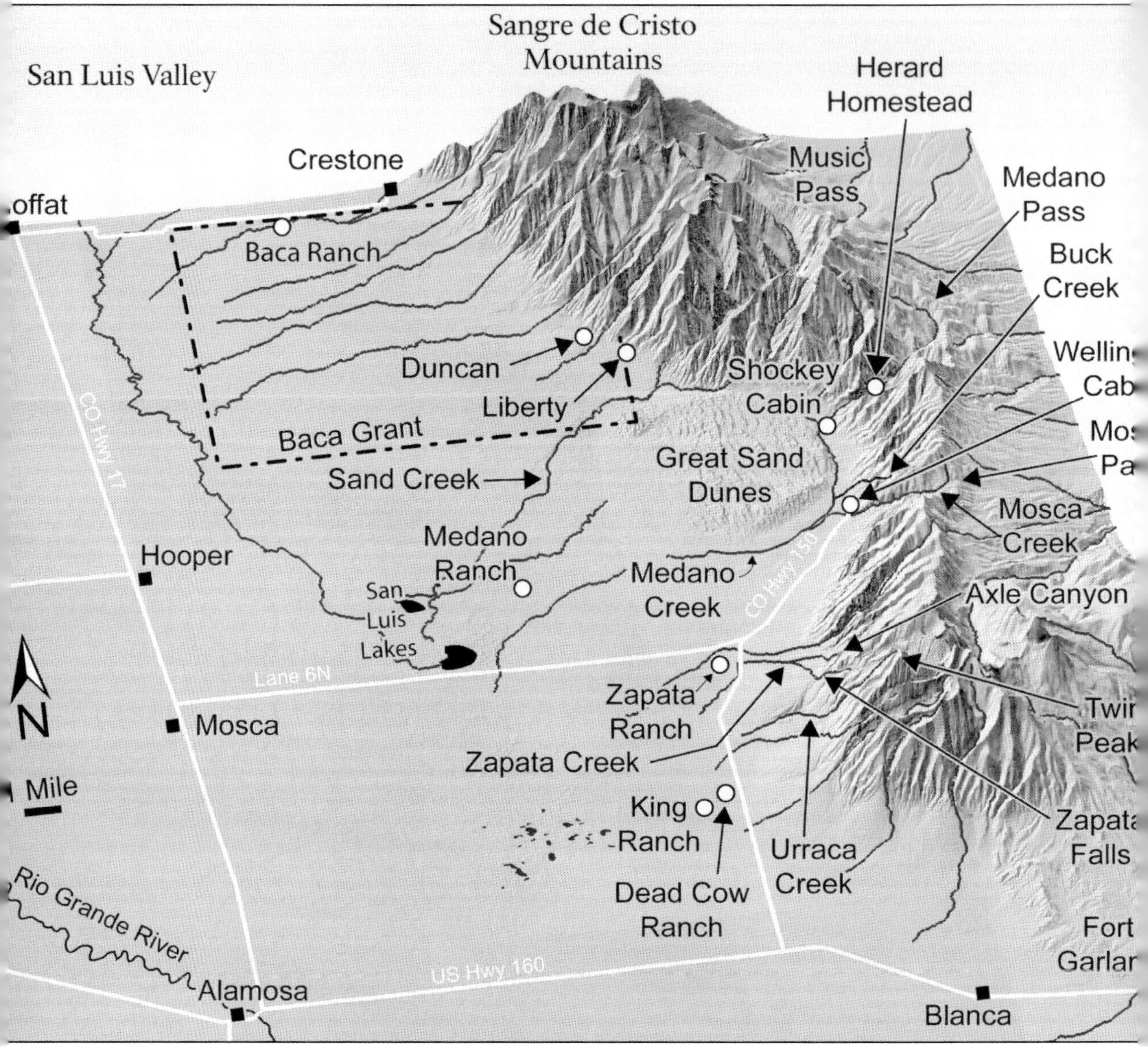

San Luis Valley Location Map. Virtually all of the places discussed in this book can be located on this map. For a map of the component segments of Great Sand Dunes National Park & Preserve, see page 116. (Map by Andrew Valdez; courtesy GRSA.)

One

Mountains, Sand, Wind, and Water Form Dunes

Gazing upon the huge piles of sand stacked up against the Sangre de Cristo Mountains, the obvious question for every visitor is: "Where did they come from?" After all, this is a mountain valley, not a desert or a seashore where one might expect dunes. To the west of the San Luis Valley, the San Juan Mountains are of volcanic origin. Erosion of those rocks creates sand particles, which are carried east by water to the San Luis Valley and are then blown by the prevailing southwesterly winds to pile up against the blockading Sangre de Cristo Mountains. Another source of sand is the erosive action of swift mountain streams, such as Sand Creek and Medano Creek, which bring sand westward from the Sangre de Cristos. Primarily quartzite in origin, this sand is deposited at the base of the dunes and blown back onto them by the southwesterly winds.

Thus, wind and water are the key elements in the formation of the dunes with the mountain ranges on the west and east providing source rock for the sand particles. Furthermore, the mountains on the east, the Sangre de Cristos, block the sand from being blown any farther east, and the dunes are formed where the southwesterly wind is funneled through three mountain passes: Music Pass, Medano Pass, and Mosca Pass (from north to south). Sometimes, there are northeasterly winds, which tend to blow the dunes back upon themselves, preventing further encroachment eastward.

Geologists estimate the dunes to be about 12,000 years old. They are part of a four-fold ecological system shown in the diagram on the following page—the watershed (the streams of the Sangre de Cristos, which bring sand westward), the dunefield (the highest dunes, reaching over 700 feet high), the sand sheet (an area of sand not fully gathered into dunes, held fairly stable by vegetation), and the *sabkha* (an area of shallow lakes that are formed from the fluctuating water table and which, when dried up, leave behind an alkaline, crusty soil). Geologists are constantly studying these ecosystems and how the various parts interact with each other.

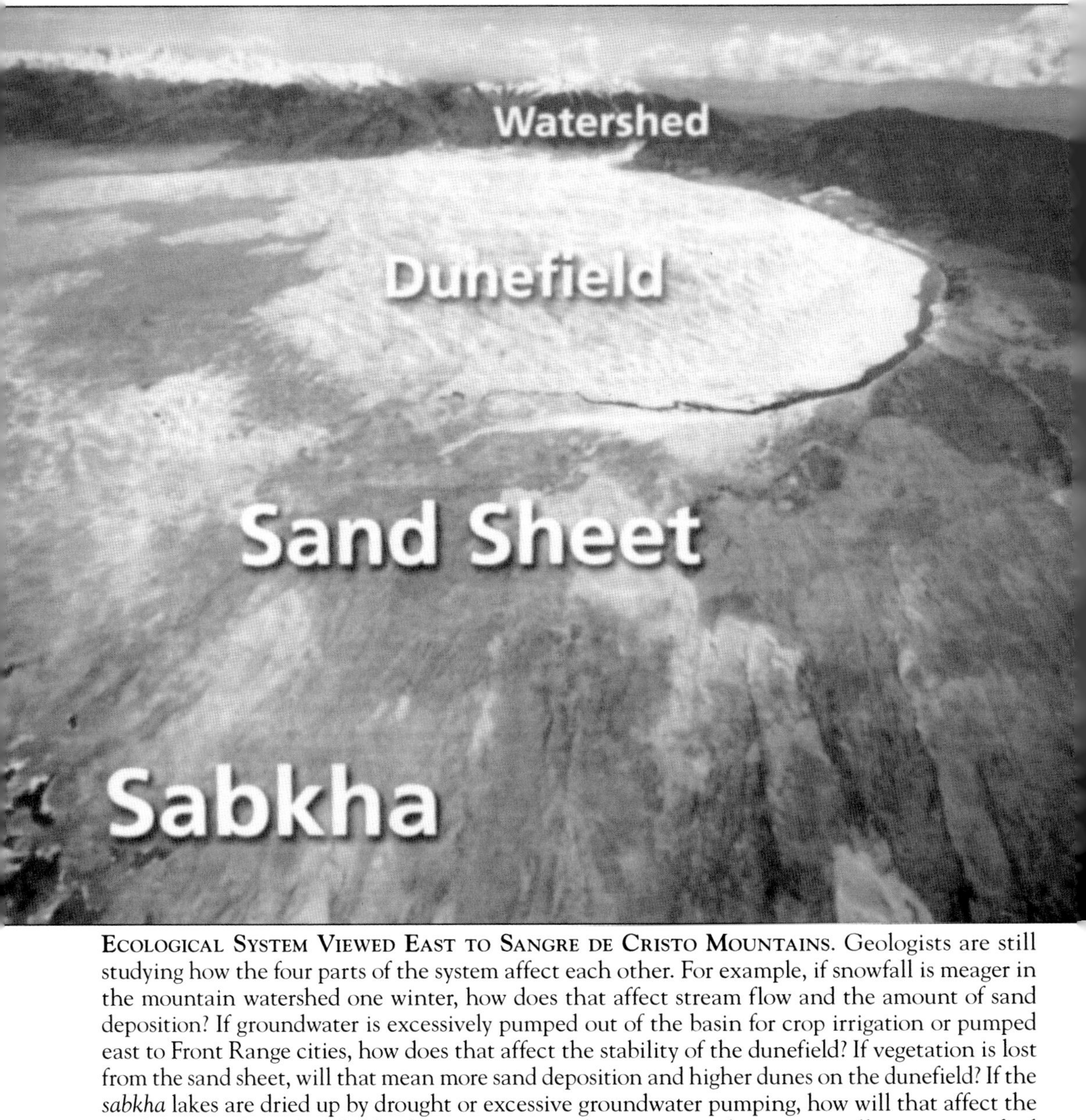

ECOLOGICAL SYSTEM VIEWED EAST TO SANGRE DE CRISTO MOUNTAINS. Geologists are still studying how the four parts of the system affect each other. For example, if snowfall is meager in the mountain watershed one winter, how does that affect stream flow and the amount of sand deposition? If groundwater is excessively pumped out of the basin for crop irrigation or pumped east to Front Range cities, how does that affect the stability of the dunefield? If vegetation is lost from the sand sheet, will that mean more sand deposition and higher dunes on the dunefield? If the *sabkha* lakes are dried up by drought or excessive groundwater pumping, how will that affect the sand sheet and the dunefield? This is a very complex system, and scientists will continue to find answers to these and other questions as further studies are conducted. The purpose of the creation of Great Sand Dunes National Park & Preserve was to protect this entire ecosystem. (GRSA.)

"The Lake and the Sand Hills." This sketch, done by Samuel Richardson on Wednesday, October 9, 1872, is one of the first recorded drawings of the Great Sand Dunes. The dunes appear left of center, below the peaks, with water (noted as "the lake") below the dunes. At the top is written, "This is the way through the Mosca Pass." (GRSA.)

Great Sand Dunes, 1874. This image by frontier photographer William Henry Jackson is the first known photograph of the dunes. Medano Creek appears to be dry at the base of the dunes, indicating a late-summer or fall time frame. The twin-peak mountain at the upper right is Cleveland Peak with an elevation of 13,414 feet. (GRSA.)

Enlargement of William Henry Jackson's 1874 Photograph. An amazing similarity in the general shape of the Great Sand Dunes is shown in these two photographs, taken 137 years apart.

National Park Service Photograph, 2011. The similarity of the three hills reflects the overall stability of the dunefield over a long period of time. Opposing wind directions (southwest/northeast)

The same three hills are shown in each photograph with Cleveland Peak to the right. (GRSA.)

along the mountain front are the main reason for the dunes stability. Lower down their slope, the dunes show more diversity in wave patterns. (GRSA.)

"SAND HILLS WEST END, 1919." Photographer Ory T. (O.T.) Davis took some of the first known photographs of the Great Sand Dunes after William Henry Jackson. Davis, from Iowa, originally tried copper mining on Pass Creek, east of the Sangre de Cristos. When the mines played out, he moved to Walsenburg and started a commercial photography business. (MVHS.)

"MADANA AND SAND HILL, 1919." This O.T. Davis photograph captures the view farther east from the one above. Davis labeled Medano Creek "Madana" based upon local pronunciation. He had, by this time, moved his photography business west from the Walsenburg/La Veta area to Alamosa, which is the nearest large town to the Great Sand Dunes. (MVHS.)

Road to Great Sand Dunes, 1927. The primitive, two-track road seen in the mid-foreground of this Wilhelm family photograph shows how difficult it was to drive a vehicle to the dunes in 1927. This northward view shows the jagged Crestone Peaks to the left, Cleveland Peak in the center, and Mount Herard to the right, all rising high above the dunes. (GRSA-5594.)

Mount Seven and the Dunes, 1931. This Wilhelm photograph shows the Great Sand Dunes one year before they becamc a national monument in 1932. Mount Seven towers above the dunes at an elevation of 13,297 feet. In 1984, it was renamed Mount Herard in honor of the pioneering Herard family of Medano Canyon. (GRSA-747.)

Windmill at the Outpost, 1974. Wind and water are the two main factors contributing to the formation of the Great Sand Dunes. Southwesterly winds blow sand across the San Luis Valley to the dunefield. This windmill used wind power to pump water up to the outpost, located just south of today's Sand Dunes Oasis campground and store. (GRSA.)

Wind on the Dunes, 1961. Robert Haugen took this dramatic photograph of the wind blowing a woman's scarf on the dunes. Blowing sand is visible at her feet. While dune ridges are shifting all the time, the dunefield itself is stabilized by opposing primary wind directions. (GRSA-5602.)

STEAM POWERED IRRIGATION DITCH DIGGER, 1912. O.T. Davis shot this photograph on the plains east of Hooper. Water (both groundwater and flowing streams) is another major factor in the formation of the Great Sand Dunes. Water is also essential to irrigation of farms in the San Luis Valley. Here, this ditch digger is hard at work as members of the Alamosa Boosters Club look on. (MVHS.)

IRRIGATION DITCH NEAR HOOPER, 1911. This O.T. Davis view looks east toward the Sangre de Cristo Mountains with the Great Sand Dunes visible as a light blur at the base of the mountains. Irrigated crops in the San Luis Valley include potatoes, sugar beets, and beans. (MVHS.)

IRRIGATION DITCH EAST OF MOSCA, C. 1912. This completed irrigation ditch in O.T. Davis's photograph illustrates the dependence of crops in the dry San Luis Valley upon groundwater pumped to the canals. The view looks east toward the Blanca massif of the Sangre de Cristo Mountains. (MVHS.)

IRRIGATION DITCH EAST OF MOSCA, 2012. A century later, the huge ditches still carry water across the San Luis Valley. This view is just south of San Luis Lake State Park, looking west toward the Great Sand Dunes and Mosca Pass (seen as the low point on the mountain ridge). Excessive groundwater pumping is now seen as a threat to the dunes.

WILLIAM GEORGE RANCH NEAR ALAMOSA, 1912. Photographer O.T. Davis was on hand to capture this scene of an automobile about to cross a bridge over an irrigation ditch in the San Luis Valley. The Sangre de Cristo Mountains can be seen in the background. (MVHS.)

"PRARIE DITCH" NEAR MOSCA, 1912. Automobile passengers cooled their heels at the irrigation ditch as O.T. Davis took their photograph. Mosca is the nearest town to the Great Sand Dunes and is the official mailing address for the national park. (MVHS.)

Water Reflection, c. 1962. Water is the lifeblood of the Great Sand Dunes and the San Luis Valley. Mount Herard and the dunes are captured here in the reflection of this temporary pool of water.

Medano Creek Bed, October 1951. When Medano Creek dries up, it is easy to see the massive quantities of sand it has brought down from the Sangre de Cristos. This sand is then blown back onto the dune piles by the prevailing southwesterly winds. Mountains, sand, wind, and water are the natural elements in dune creation. (GRSA-2300.)

Two

American Indians, Explorers, and Mountain Passes

Three mountain passes cross the Sangre de Cristos leading westward to the Great Sand Dunes. The elevation decreases from north to south, from Music Pass, to Medano Pass, to Mosca Pass. So it was natural that the two southern passes (Medano and Mosca) were most used by American Indians, explorers, and settlers. Just south of Great Sand Dunes, archeological excavations have revealed that prehistoric hunter-gatherers occupied the area between about 11,000 and 10,000 years ago. Their projectile points (Clovis points and Folsom points) indicate their skill in carving stone points to hunt mammoth and bison. The historic Ute tribe used horses captured from the Spanish conquistadors to become the dominant tribe in the area, crossing the mountain passes for trade and hunting.

Lt. Zebulon Pike of the US Army was the first recorded American explorer to cross the Sangre de Cristos to the Great Sand Dunes. Pike and his men were exploring the Louisiana Purchase territory under orders from Pres. Thomas Jefferson. In January 1807, they crossed either Medano or Mosca Pass (they did not know where they were and left no accurate description of the pass), and Pike recorded seeing the dunes in his journal. Later, explorers John Charles Fremont (in 1848) and Capt. John Gunnison (in 1853) crossed the passes searching for a suitable rail route for the transcontinental railroad. Neither Medano nor Mosca Pass was suitable for a railroad, but Mosca Pass became an important wagon road to the San Luis Valley in the 1870s.

In 1871, Frank Hastings received a charter from the Colorado Territorial Legislature to build and maintain a toll road over Mosca Pass. The community of Montville was established at the location of Hastings's general store and toll gate at the west end of the Mosca Pass Road. This location can be viewed in Great Sand Dunes National Park today on the trail leading from the Montville parking lot to Mosca Pass. Traffic was heavy over Mosca Pass with as many as 40 wagons crossing in a day. Montville boomed with a total of about 20 houses and a post office located in the general store.

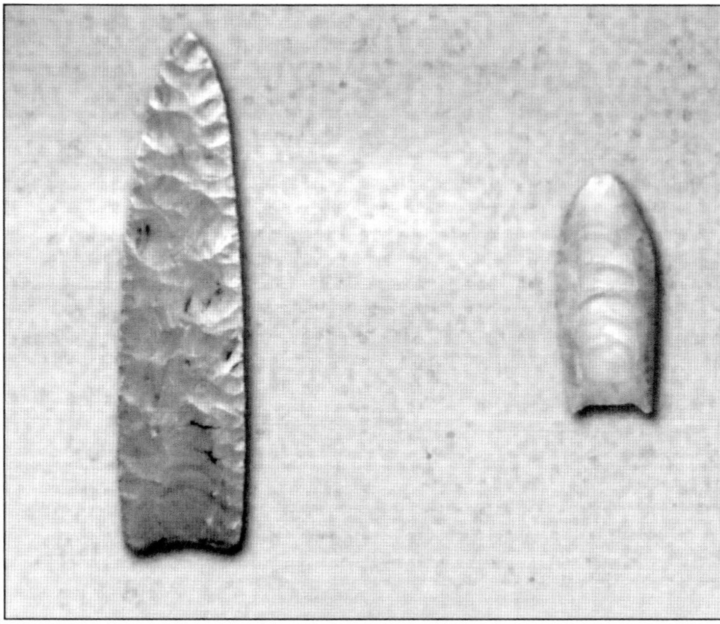

Clovis and Folsom Projectile Points. Clovis points (left) were found just south of the Great Sand Dunes in 1979, along with mammoth bone and ivory. The Clovis culture has been dated to 11,000 years ago. Folsom points (right), along with the remains of 35 bison, were found from between 1981 and 1983 at an excavation on the Zapata Ranch south of the dunes and were dated to about 10,000 years ago. (GRSA.)

Great Sand Dunes Arrowheads. In 1958, park superintendent Harold Schaafsma displayed these arrowheads donated by area ranchers. Mostly from the Ute tribe, the arrowheads were found by the hundreds on ranches surrounding the dunes. Many were found at Indian Spring, in what is now the southwest portion of the park. Today, removal of arrowheads and artifacts from national parks is prohibited. (GRSA-2157.)

Utes on Horseback. After securing horses from Spanish explorers and conquistadors during the 1600s, the Utes became very adept in using horses for hunting and fighting. By the 1800s, they were the dominant American Indian tribe from the San Luis Valley east to the Spanish Peaks. (GRSA.)

Culturally Peeled Pine Trees. Over 100 scarred ponderosa pine trees have been found in Great Sand Dunes. Tree ring dating has revealed that the lower bark of these trees was peeled off between 1815 and 1846, when the Ute tribe dominated the area. The interior bark layer was eaten, suggesting the scarcity of buffalo and other big game by this time period. The bark was also used for medicinal purposes. (GRSA.)

Portrait of Lt. Zebulon Montgomery Pike. After crossing Medano (or perhaps Mosca) Pass in January 1807, Pike came upon the Great Sand Dunes and, according to his journal, "ascended one of the highest hills of sand and with [his] glass could discover a large river flowing nearly north by west and south by east through the plain." Pike was looking at the Rio Grande River. (Independence National Historic Site.)

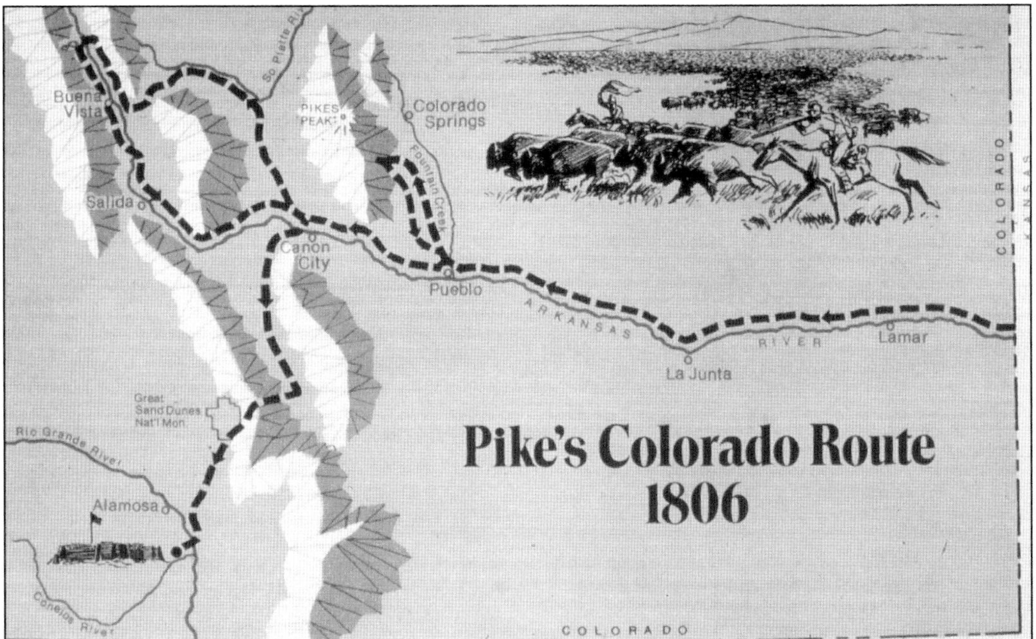

Pike's Journey, 1806–1807. Zebulon Pike explored the area north of Pueblo in 1806, reaching the base (but not the summit) of Pikes Peak. He then made a loop northwest from the Canon City area before heading southwest over the Sangre de Cristo Mountains to the Great Sand Dunes. He built a rough defensive stockade near the confluence of the Rio Grande and Conejos Rivers. (GRSA.)

Pike's Stockade, 1977. In 1952, the Colorado Historical Society reconstructed Pike's stockade near its original location at the confluence of the Rio Grande and Conejos Rivers. Here, in February 1807, Pike and his men were captured by Spanish soldiers and sent as prisoners to Mexico. They were later released on US soil, and Pike was killed in 1813 while fighting against the British in the continuing War of 1812. (GRSA.)

Pike's "Sand Hills." In his journal, Pike noted that "the sand hills extended up and down at the foot of the White Mountains (Sangre de Cristos) and appeared to be about five miles in width." The "sand hills" were covered in a couple of inches of snow in this scene from the Visitor Center, May 10, 2012.

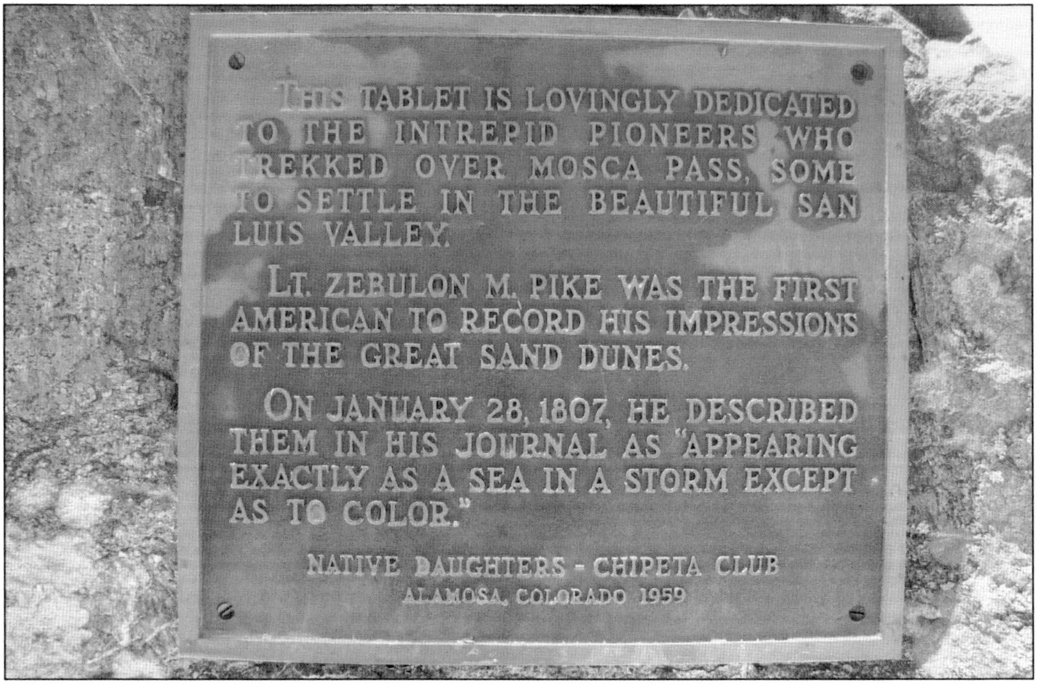

Marker at Montville on Mosca Pass Trail. Frank Hastings constructed his toll road over Mosca Pass in 1871, and a small settlement grew up at its western terminus at the base of the Great Sand Dunes. Known variously as "Mosco," "Monteville," and, finally, "Montville," the settlement included 20 homes and Hastings's general store/toll cabin.

Old Tollgate Cabin at Western Foot of Mosca Pass. This 1927 photograph shows Walter and Ada (Wellington) Holeman posing in front of the ruins of the Mosca Pass tollgate cabin at Montville. Ada was the daughter of William Wellington, a pioneer settler at Uracca. She was also the sister of Frank Wellington, who built the Wellington cabin, which still stands in Great Sand Dunes National Park. (GRSA-731.)

Mosca Pass Toll Road. This 1968 booklet cover illustrates the toll cabin at Montville with a team of oxen pulling a covered wagon up the road. In the background, the Great Sand Dunes can be seen with Mount Herard rising above them. Tolls were 50¢ per head of livestock, $1 for a horse and rider, and $2 for a team and wagon.

Montville Area, Mosca Pass Trail, 1989. This view east at Montville illustrates how the toll area operated with a fence across Mosca Creek, forcing wagons and riders to stay on the road and pay at the toll cabin, which was on the left. The Mosca Pass road was obliterated by a flood in 1911 and never reopened. (GRSA-2183.)

Sand Dunes Rise above Montville Parking Lot, 1958. The Montville Post Office operated in the general store building from February 28, 1887, until January 31, 1900. Montville was abandoned not long after the road over Mosca Pass was closed in 1911. This parking lot was built by the National Park Service for hikers on the Mosca Pass Trail. Paved in 1964, it still serves today. (GRSA-2160.)

Medano Pass Entrance to Great Sand Dunes. The Medano Pass Road, north of Mosca Pass, is still open to four-wheel drive vehicles. Steeper and higher in elevation, it crosses more treacherous sand areas than the Mosca Pass Trail. Wagon drivers preferred Mosca Pass, while individual riders could bypass tolls by using Medano Pass.

Three

Settlers and Ranchers around the Dunes

The Homestead Act, passed by Congress in 1862, opened the American West to settlers, particularly after the Civil War ended in 1865. A settler could obtain 160 acres of federal land by filing a claim, living on and improving the land for five years, and then filing for a deed on the property. In the area around the Great Sand Dunes, settlement was a mixture of Hispanic and Anglo (including Mormon) homesteaders, plus leftover owners from Mexican land grants, and large ranches financed by easterners that sometimes bought out the homesteaders or took over their land by force.

Hispanic settler Teofilo Trujillo claimed land southwest of Indian Spring in 1865 and started a cattle and sheep ranch. His son Pedro also claimed land nearby in 1879 and built a ranch house by 1885. Pedro's log home has been restored and was added to the National Register of Historic Places in 2004. Unfortunately, his father Teofilo's ranch house was burned down in 1902 by local cattle operators, and both Trujillo families sold their land and moved out of the area.

Mexican land grants in the area were declared invalid by Colorado's surveyor general in 1874, and Hispanic settlers on the grants sold their land to large ranches such as the nearby Zapata Ranch, just south of the Great Sand Dunes, and the Medano Ranch, just west of the dunes. However, the Baca Grant of 100,000 acres north of the Great Sand Dunes was validated for the Baca family in 1864 by the surveyor general of the Colorado Territory. The Bacas immediately deeded the grant to their lawyer, and the ranch went through a series of many owners over the years. When it was finally purchased by the Nature Conservancy in 2004, part of it was included in Great Sand Dunes National Park, about one third went to the US Forest Service, and the remainder formed the newly created Baca National Wildlife Refuge. Also, not to be forgotten are the Mormon homesteaders who settled on Uracca Creek, just south of the dunes, many of whose descendants still live in the San Luis Valley.

TEOFILO TRUJILLO AND HIS GRANDCHILDREN, 1901. Teofilo and his wife, Andrellita, homesteaded southwest of Indian Spring in 1865. His son Pedro and daughter-in-law Sofia homesteaded nearby in 1879. In this image, two of Pedro's children, Frederico (left) and Maria Elena (right) pose with Teofilo. Frederico was born in 1889, and Maria in 1897. (Maria Lujan Causby.)

PEDRO TRUJILLO, C. 1890. Pedro homesteaded near his father, Teofilo, but unlike his father, he raised only cattle, not sheep. Since sheep deprive cattle of grass to graze on, Teofilo's sheep ranching raised the ire of local cattle ranchers, and they were suspected of burning down his ranch house in 1902. Teofilo and Pedro both subsequently sold their ranches to the Medano Ranch and moved farther away in the San Luis Valley. (Maria Lujan Causby.)

Pedro Trujillo and Hay Wagon, c. 1890. Over time, Pedro added more land to his homestead, eventually amassing over 500 acres. Pedro grew hay on the ranch to feed his cattle. It was a fairly successful operation, and Pedro and his wife, Sofia, had 16 children (nine boys and seven girls). (Maria Lujan Causby.)

Sofia Trujillo and Grandson Benito Martinez, 1936. Pedro Trujillo was married to Sofia Maria Martinez in 1885. They had nine children on their Medano homestead, and then seven more after they sold the homestead in 1902 and moved northwest of Monte Vista. Benito was the son of their daughter Epiphania and Frederico Martinez. Epiphania (Fanny) was a cook at the Zapata Ranch for the Linger family, and Frederico (Fred) was a foreman at the Zapata Ranch. (Maria Lujan Causby.)

Restored Pedro Trujillo Home, 2012. Pedro Trujillo built a log home on his ranch in 1885, one of the few Hispanic settlers to use log construction instead of adobe. In 2012, Pedro's granddaughter Maria Lujan Causby (center) visited the home with her grandson Jerry Paul Causby Jr. (left) and her brother Armenio Lujan (right). Maria and Armenio are the children of Andrea Trujillo Lujan, one of Pedro and Sofia's seven daughters. (GRSA.)

Uracca Cemetery, 2012. Mormon families settled in the Uracca valley in the foothills of the Sangre de Cristo Mountains, overlooking the Great Sand Dunes and San Luis Valley. Several graves of the pioneering Wellington family are located here. William Wellington built a sawmill on Zapata Creek, two miles north of this location, and his son Charles operated a sawmill on Sawmill Creek, just east of Great Sand Dunes.

Uracca Valley, 2012. The Uracca (sometimes spelled *Urraca* or *Euracca*) valley was homesteaded by Mormon settlers in the 1870s and 1880s. Today, at Milepost 9 on Highway 150, just south of the Great Sand Dunes, the Uracca Road heads east into the mountains to the cemetery. Uracca Creek flows west out of the valley, seen in the center of the photograph with the Twin Peaks on the right.

Remains of Uracca Schoolhouse, c. 1960s. The Uracca School District was formed in 1888 with Nellie Calkins as the teacher. Among the first settlers in Uracca in 1871 were the following families: Leggit, Ranson, King, Land, Denton, Bailey, Orton, Calkins, Chadwell, Rumsey and Sealy. Wiley King was the presiding elder of the local Mormon church. (GRSA.)

ZAPATA FALLS, FEBRUARY 5, 1908. Two miles north of Uracca Creek, Zapata Creek becomes a frozen waterfall as it cascades down the canyon in winter. William Wellington's sawmill processed timber harvested along Zapata Creek. The wood was then used for railroad ties, bridge timbers, and homes in the San Luis Valley. (MVHS.)

ZAPATA RANCH HOUSE CONSTRUCTION. A couple of miles northwest of Zapata Falls, the Dickey brothers brought in cattle herds from Texas, establishing the Zapata Ranch in 1876. They purchased the land from Hispanic settlers whose Mexican land grant claims were denied in 1874. In this photograph, Albert and Genevieve Linger oversee construction of a new Zapata ranch house in 1928. (GRSA.)

Finished Zapata Ranch House, c. 1928. The early Zapata Ranch was a stage stop and a post office with the post office operating from 1879 to 1900. The Dickey brothers sold the ranch in 1882 to New York investors Adee and Durkee. Eventually, the combined Medano-Zapata Ranch was purchased by George W. Linger in 1912, and his family operated it until 1947. (GRSA.)

Zapata Ranch House, 2012. The original structure, with three dormer windows on the roof, can be seen in the center of the photograph. The later additions included lodging and a dining room. The Nature Conservancy bought the combined Medano-Zapata Ranch (over 100,000 acres) in 1999 for $6.5 million, and the Medano Ranch portion is now part of Great Sand Dunes National Park.

MEDANO RANCH AND GREAT SAND DUNES. Directly west of the Great Sand Dunes, brothers Valentine and William Dickey established the Medano Ranch in the early 1870s, prior to their purchase of the Zapata Ranch in 1876. The brothers sold their beef at the Dickey Meat Market, operated by William in the mining town of Leadville, to the north. Valentine, meanwhile, operated the ranch. (GRSA.)

MEDANO RANCH HEADQUARTERS. In April 1877, Valentine Dickey constructed a one-room log house, which became the headquarters of the Medano Ranch. A post office called Medano Springs was opened there in June 1877 with William Dickey as postmaster. This later photograph shows the considerable expansion of the ranch buildings by the Linger family. (GRSA.)

MEDANO RANCH WAGONS AND WATCHTOWER. In the 1870s and 1880s, raids by Ute Indians upon San Luis Valley ranches were rare but still a potential threat. The Medano Ranch operators constructed a tall watchtower (to the left in the photograph) to keep an eye out for roaming bands of Ute raiders. (GRSA.)

MEDANO RANCH WATCHTOWER. Ranch hands stop for a drink of cool water from an irrigation pipe below the Indian watchtower. When George W. Linger purchased the Medano-Zapata Ranch in 1912 for $200,000, he obtained 12,948 deeded acres, 52,500 acres of leased state land, and water rights in 10 irrigation ditches. (GRSA.)

FORTY THOUSAND POUNDS OF WOOD CROSS SAN LUIS VALLEY, 1908. In this O.T. Davis photograph, G.W. Winner and his son haul six wagonloads of wood behind their powerful steam tractor, heading west toward the town of Mosca. The Great Sand Dunes and Sangre de Cristo Mountains can be seen faintly in the background. Also note the horse-drawn chuck wagon at the rear. (MVHS.)

TWENTY-FIVE HORSEPOWER CROSS-COMPOUND REEVES TRACTION ENGINE, 1908. Wood was a precious commodity in the largely treeless San Luis Valley. Settlers needed wood for fence posts, homes, and fuel, so cut timber was hauled west from the Sangre de Cristo Mountains across the sandy plains. This location is actually about 20 miles west of Mosca Pass, near the town of Mosca. (MVHS.)

MOSCA FARMERS' ELEVATOR COMPANY, 1912. The Denver & Rio Grande (D&RG) Railroad opened a narrow-gauge rail line from Villa Grove at the north end of the San Luis Valley to Alamosa in November 1890. Small towns immediately sprang up along the line, including Mosca, Hooper, and Moffat. The railroad encouraged these settlements in order to build up freight revenue along the line. (MVHS.)

MOSCA FARMERS' ELEVATOR COMPANY STOCK CERTIFICATE, OCTOBER 1, 1898. Wood hauler G.W. Winner owned six shares in the Mosca Farmers' Elevator Company. The tall elevator building stored wheat, which was milled into flour and then shipped out on the D&RG Railroad. The railroad also encouraged San Luis Valley farmers to grow potatoes, onions, carrots, and sugar beets. (MVHS.)

MOSCA SCHOOL, 1912. This O.T. Davis photograph captures children playing at recess at the Mosca School, which had 12 grades. The town of Mosca and Mosca Pass (located about 20 miles to the east) may have been named after *mosca*, the Spanish word for "fly," the predominant irritating insect in the Great Sand Dunes area. (MVHS.)

FRED GOSS POTATO FARM NEAR HOOPER, 1911. Potatoes were, and still are, the major crop of the San Luis Valley. This O.T. Davis photograph looks east toward the Great Sand Dunes (the white line at base of Sangre de Cristo Mountains). Hooper was named for Maj. Shadrach K. Hooper, the general passenger and ticket agent for the D&RG Railroad. (MVHS.)

HOOPER HOT SPRINGS POOL, C. 1940. In *Sand Stories*, Emmett Calkins, a Zapata ranch hand, says of the pool in the 1920s, "Them farmers just went in there with teams and horses and dug out a big pit there, and that water come out of there—it was hot! Boy, I mean it could cook you when it come out of the ground." (MVHS.)

MOFFAT MAIN STREET, 1913. Luther and Bessye Gross are pictured showing off their new car on an otherwise deserted Main Street in Moffat. Moffat was named for David H. Moffat, president of the D&RG Railroad when the line was built through the area in 1890. (MVHS.)

Entrance Gate, Baca National Wildlife Refuge, 2012. When the Nature Conservancy purchased and transferred the Baca Ranch to the federal government in 2004, it marked the end of a long line of owners that began with the Luis Maria Baca family in 1864. The eastern section of the ranch became part of Great Sand Dunes National Park & Preserve, while the western section became the wildlife refuge.

Baca Ranch Headquarters, February 2005. With over 100,000 acres, the Baca Ranch was one of the largest cattle ranches in the San Luis Valley. In the summer, the large ranches often drove their cattle to the railhead in Hooper, where cattle were loaded onto cattle cars and shipped to northern New Mexico. There, they were unloaded and allowed to graze and fatten on the lush mountain meadows near Cumbres Pass. (GRSA.)

Four

The Herard Family

One of the legendary pioneer families around the Great Sand Dunes was the Herard family. Jean Francois Herard was born in France in January 1833. His wife, Julia Babey, was born in Switzerland in April 1841. The family immigrated to the United States, and their son Ulysses (nicknamed "Ulus") was born in Independence, Missouri, on July 20, 1859. His sister Euphrasie was born in Kansas on September 15, 1861, and died June 27, 1872. In 1872, the family left Kansas, crossing the plains in a wagon to the San Luis Valley. They settled near Deadman's Creek in what is now the northern portion of Great Sand Dunes National Park. After three years of homesteading, they were unable to obtain title to their land because they had unknowingly settled on the Baca Grant. In 1875, the family moved south to Medano Canyon and built a log cabin, blacksmith shop, and corrals just a mile and a half up Medano Creek from the current national park boundary.

When traveling the Medano Pass Primitive Road today in a four-wheel drive vehicle, the remoteness and ruggedness of the canyon can easily be observed. Here, the Herard family raised cattle and horses and even developed a trout fish hatchery near the creek. They hunted wild game, including deer and bear. Mountain lions were "great calf-killers," so Ulus continually set traps for them, supposedly killing 100 or more in his lifetime. In 1888, Ulus married Mary Frances Dickenson, and their daughter Julia Virginia Herard was born January 30, 1889. A post office officially named Herard was established in their home from 1905 to 1912, and Mary Frances was the postmistress.

Ulus's father died in 1892, and his mother died in 1897. His wife left him in 1913, after the post office closed. He lived alone in the canyon until his poor health forced his daughter to seek hospital treatment for him in Pueblo, Colorado, in 1937; he died there on September 27, 1940. Though he lived alone, Ulus was constantly visited by hunting parties and his many friends. He also frequently saw his daughter Julia, son-in-law John W. Williams, and grandsons Bill and Jack.

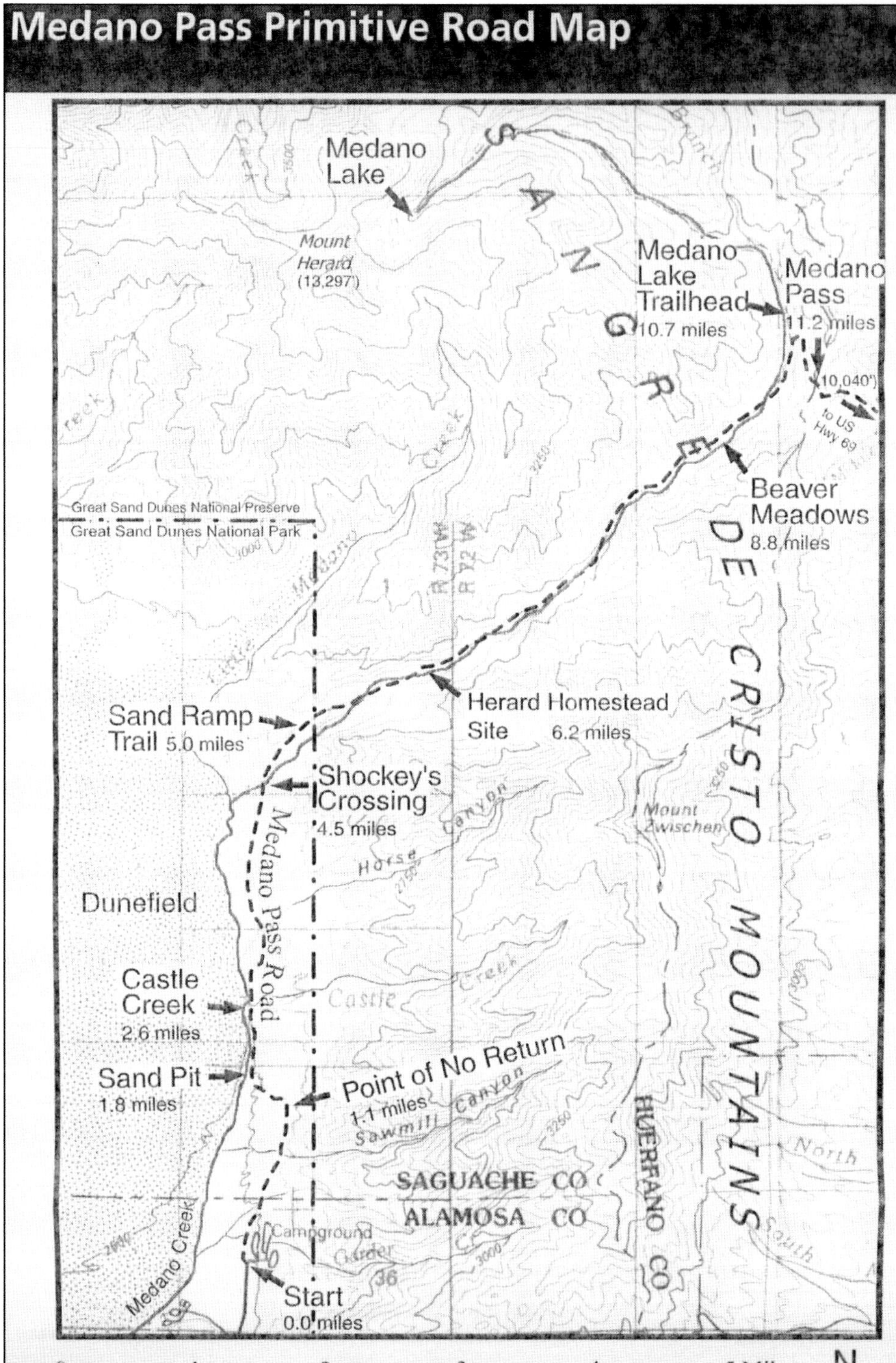

MEDANO PASS PRIMITIVE ROAD. It is 11.2 miles from the start of the road up to Medano Pass. When the sand is dry, tires on four-wheel drive vehicles must be deflated at the Point of No Return; otherwise, vehicles will become stuck in the deep sand. (GRSA.)

Jean Francois Herard, c. 1880. Life in Medano Canyon proved difficult for the Herards, and Jean Francois passed away in 1892 at the age of 59. His wife, Julia, died in 1897 at the age of 56. Both were buried in Medano Canyon but were later moved to a legal cemetery in Alamosa. (GRSA-5290.)

Herard Ranch, Medano Canyon, 1892. Timber was abundant in the canyon and provided a sturdy log home for the Herards. Seated at the left is Jean Francois Herard, and to the far right is his wife, Julia Babey Herard. The little girl in the center is Ulysses Herard's daughter, Julia. The two men are unidentified. (GRSA-5265.)

Herard Ranch, 1894. Seated on the porch is Ulysses Herard. When he was about 20 years old, he was thrown off his horse and kicked in the head, rendering him deaf in both ears. For the rest of his life, he used a long cow horn as a hearing aid, and he also relied heavily on paper and pencil for communication. (GRSA-5289.)

Ulysses Herard at His Medano Canyon Homestead, 1904. Many stories are told about Ulus, including one about the time he was rounding up cattle near Medano Pass when he came between a mother bear and her two cubs. The mother charged him, and he fired his pistol, but it jammed. He eluded the bear and, on her next charge, pulled his axe from his belt and killed her. (GRSA-5449.)

Herard Blacksmith Shop, c. 1904. Ulus Herard (right) was well known for his hospitality; if he was not home, travelers were welcome to use his cabin, food, and firewood. He only asked that the dishes were washed and the firewood restocked. The other man in this image is unidentified. (GRSA-5287.)

Herard Cattle Corral. While Ulus did have this corral at his ranch house, most of the time his cattle roamed free on unfenced land from Medano Pass to the Great Sand Dunes. When the cattle were ready for market, he herded them to the railhead at Hooper or Alamosa. (GRSA-5286.)

ULUS AND FRIENDS, C. 1930. Despite living alone since his wife left him, Ulus never lacked companionship. He was visited by a constant stream of friends from all around. Here, he enjoys a campfire meal with two unidentified women at his ranch. (GRSA-5264.)

A GOOD DAY OF FISHING, C. 1930. Ulus and his maternal cousin Frances Babey had a great day catching trout in Medano Creek. Of course, the creek was well stocked from the trout hatchery on his ranch. Frances Babey was from Pueblo, Colorado, where Ulus went when he had to leave the canyon in ill health in 1937. (GRSA-5283.)

Deer Hunting in Medano Canyon. Ulus was an accomplished hunter, and game was abundant in Medano Canyon. His grandson Jack Williams reported that Ulus was a great cook—especially of venison and beef. Ulus also taught himself taxidermy, preserving the best specimens from his hunts. (GRSA-5272.)

Medano Canyon Hunting Party. Ulus (second from right) often led hunting parties in the canyon; this one was quite successful with a bag of four deer and a bear. Elk had long vanished from the canyon, and through 1948, Jack Williams said that he had never seen an elk there. (GRSA-5282.)

Ulus Herard on the Great Sand Dunes, c. 1930. Ulus (center) met these unidentified gents on the dunes and undoubtedly gave them a guided tour. Besides cattle ranching and hunting, Jack Williams said that Ulus was obsessed with striking it rich, and he prospected all over the mountain canyons, digging little holes all around. (GRSA-5271.)

On the Dunes, c. 1930. Ulus Herard leads Mrs. Frances Babey (riding his white mule Neddy) on a tour of the dunes. Ulus had to renew his cattle-grazing leases in the national forest periodically, so he often rode Neddy east over Medano Pass to the Gardner office of forest ranger Paul Gilbert Sr. They became good friends, and Gilbert was a pallbearer at Ulus's funeral. (GRSA-5281.)

Last Known Photograph of Ulysses Herard. This may have been taken in Pueblo, where Ulus lived from 1937 until his death in 1940. The "Frenchman," as he was known, had lived quite a life of adventure in Medano Canyon. He was always remembered for his friendship and hospitality, which was reciprocated when he stayed overnight with friends in Gardner, Liberty, and other places around the Great Sand Dunes. (GRSA-5279.)

Julia Virginia Herard, c. 1891. Julia was the only child of Ulysses Herard and Mary Frances Dickenson. She grew up on the Herard Ranch in Medano Canyon and was homeschooled by her mother for the first few years of her education. (GRSA-5269.)

Julia Herard at the Medano Canyon Ranch, 1895. After being homeschooled for several years, Julia was sent to high school in Canon City (west of Pueblo). In this photograph, she is about six years old.

Julia Herard at the Medano Canyon Ranch, 1907. Julia spent summers at the ranch while attending high school in Canon City. Her summer chores most likely included cooking; mending and washing clothes; and helping her father, Ulus, with the cattle and horses. (GRSA-5263.)

At the Herard Ranch, 1907. Pictured here are, from left to right, Julia Herard; her mother, Mary Dickenson Herard; and Julia's friend Ruth Saunders. While summers were a busy time at the ranch, the season did provide relief from the bitter, cold, snowy winters at 8,800 feet of elevation. (GRSA-5275.)

At Liberty, Colorado, 1907. Ruth Saunders (left) and Julia Herard (right) rode horses to the gold mining town of Liberty, which was about eight miles northwest of the Herard Ranch. Liberty was a boomtown, and most of the supplies the Herards needed could be purchased there. (GRSA-5270.)

Medano Creek and Great Sand Dunes, c. 1930. Mrs. Frances Babey (left) and Julia Herard (right) gaze toward the mountain peak that would later be named Mount Herard (in 1984) in honor of the Herard family. This location is near the present-day picnic-area parking lot, nearly six and a half miles southwest of the Herard Ranch. (GRSA-5280.)

Herard Family at the Ranch, c. 1930. Pictured here are, from left to right, Ulysses Herard; his daughter Julia; and her husband, John Williams. The dog's name is unknown. Julia and John had two sons, William (Bill) and Jack. Julia died in 1956. (GRSA-5278.)

Fish Fry at the Herard Ranch. This undated photograph shows a young Jack Williams (son of Julia and John and grandson of Ulysses Herard) with Frank Jackson (right). According to the inscription on the back, "Mr. Jackson once saved Mr. Herard's life." (GRSA-5284.)

Jack Williams at the Herard Ranch, c. 1940. Jack Williams recalled that, when his brother Bill was married in 1937, the newlyweds moved to the ranch from Canon City. The Herard family descendants occupied the ranch until 1948, some eight years after Ulysses Herard died in 1940. (GRSA-5273.)

HERARD RANCH FOUNDATION WALLS, 2012. Nothing is left of the several Herard Ranch buildings except for this square foundation, which can be seen just off the Medano Pass Primitive Road, about six and one-fifth miles northeast of Pinyon Flats Campground. The rugged rock walls of Medano Canyon encircle the former ranch area.

HOWARD SHOCKEY'S CABIN, 2012. Howard Shockey first came to the Great Sand Dunes in April 1926. He became a close friend of Ulysses Herard and purchased land for this cabin from Herard's son-in-law John Williams. The cabin is located at Shockey's Crossing of Medano Creek, four and a half miles north of the campground. In 1937, Shockey used his wrecker truck to pull out Jack Williams's pickup truck, which was stuck in the creek.

Five

The Wellington Family

William Wellington and his wife, Esther, came from Iowa in the 1870s and settled with other Mormon families in Uracca. The Wellingtons had four children: Frank, Charles, Elizabeth (Lizzie), and Ada. On Zapata Creek, two miles north of Uracca, William started one of the first sawmills in the San Luis Valley. His son Charles was a ranch hand at the Medano Ranch and later operated a sawmill in Sawmill Canyon, just north of today's campground in Great Sand Dunes. William's son Frank worked as a fireman for the D&RG Railroad out of Alamosa.

The story is told that, in 1888, William Wellington was a member of a party sent to Alamosa to secure an American flag, which the citizens of Uracca would raise on the northern Twin Peak for the Fourth of July. There were no flags to be had, but they did return with red, white, and blue bolts of cloth, which were sewn into a flag by Lizzie Wellington and some of the local women. On July 4th, a group of 27 people, including William Wellington and his four children, hiked to the top of the peak, hoisted the flag on a log pole, sang the national anthem, and enjoyed a very memorable picnic lunch.

William's son Frank married Virginia Miller in 1895. They had eight children—one born in Mosca, three born in Uracca, and four born in Alamosa. In 1928, Frank and his son Harold constructed three buildings just north of Mosca Creek, in what is now Great Sand Dunes National Park: a cook shack; a cabin; and a tool shed, which held tools for their mine shaft just up the hill. The Wellingtons dug an irrigation ditch from Mosca Creek toward their cabin. Today's Wellington Ditch Trail, from Montville to the campground, follows a portion of the original ditch and passes above the remains of the cabin. Other than gravestones in Uracca Cemetery, the cabin is the last remaining legacy of the Wellington family in the San Luis Valley.

William Thomas Wellington, c. 1870. William and his wife, Esther, brought their family west from Iowa in the 1870s and settled with other Mormon families in Uracca. William's sawmill on Zapata Creek produced pine planks for siding, flooring, and roofing for houses in the area. His extended family is shown in the chart below. (GRSA.)

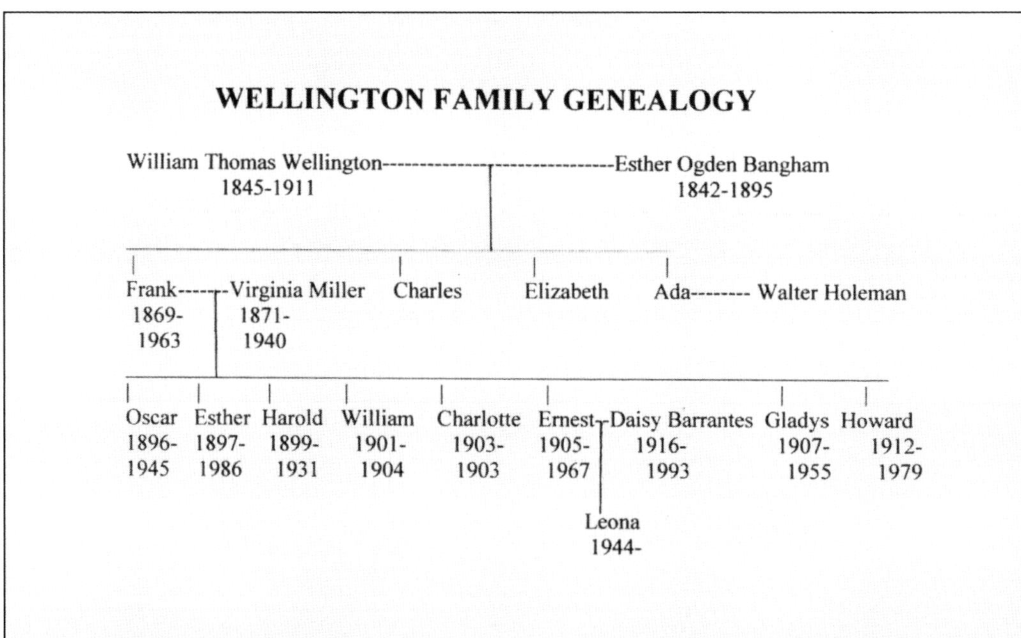

Wellington Family Genealogy. Due to space limitations, the only marriages shown are that of Frank Wellington and Virginia Miller and that of Ernest Wellington and Daisy Barrantes, since their photographs appear in the following pages. Leona Wellington, daughter of Ernest and Daisy, is the main source of this genealogy.

Sawmill Canyon, 2012. William Wellington's son Charles built a sawmill in this vicinity. Today, the National Park Service has developed a handicapped-accessible campsite here, one mile north of Pinyon Flats Campground on the Medano Pass Primitive Road.

Uracca Cemetery, 2012. William Wellington's wife, Esther, and their son Frank are buried next to each other in Uracca. Frank lived to be 94 years old and was well known in the Great Sand Dunes area.

Frank Wellington and Virginia Miller Wedding, June 30, 1895. After settling in Uracca, Frank and his wife, Virginia, moved to Alamosa about 1903. Frank worked for the D&RG Railroad for many years, retiring in 1936. He was a fireman on steam locomotives, shoveling coal into the fuel box. He earned the nickname "Old Iron Claw Wellington" because he never wore gloves when shoveling coal. (GRSA.)

Frank Wellington Family, c. 1920. Two of Frank and Virginia's children died in infancy, but the other six are pictured here with their parents. They are, from left to right, Gladys (born 1907, Alamosa), Ernest (born 1905, Alamosa), Howard (born 1912, Alamosa), Virginia, Frank, Harold (born 1899, Uracca), Esther (born 1897, Uracca), and Oscar (born 1896, Mosca). (GRSA.)

Ernest and Gladys Wellington, c. 1922. Ernest and his sister Gladys dressed up for this photograph on a celebratory occasion for Gladys. As Ernest was born in 1905, he was too young for service in World War I, and by 1940, he was too old to serve in World War II. (GRSA.)

Ernest Wellington at Dead Cow Ranch. Frank Wellington owned the Dead Cow Ranch southwest of Uracca, and Ernest worked for his father there for a number of years. Ernest inherited the ranch in 1963 when his father died. When Ernest died in 1967, the ranch went to his wife, Daisy. Daisy sold the ranch in 1969 when she moved back to her native Costa Rica. (GRSA.)

Baby Leona Wellington, c. 1946. Proud grandfather Frank Wellington (left) poses with granddaughter Leona (center) and daughter-in-law Daisy (right). Daisy married Ernest Wellington in San Jose, Costa Rica, on December 31, 1942. Their daughter Leona was born in Costa Rica in 1944, and the family moved to Alamosa at the end of World War II. (GRSA.)

Grave of Ernest Wellington in Uracca. Ernest Wellington became a civil engineer, traveling to Costa Rica in 1939 and 1940 to work on the Pan American Highway. There, he met his wife, Daisy. Their daughter Leona was born in Costa Rica in 1944, and the family moved to Alamosa a year later.

FRANK WELLINGTON AND HORSES ON THE DUNES, C. 1920S. Frank and his son Harold built a cabin just north of Mosca Creek in 1928. Frank was always concerned with obtaining water in this arid landscape, as his granddaughter Leona recalled, "Grandpa's main concern was always getting water, so he was always digging ditches to divert the water for family use or planting." (GRSA.)

WELLINGTON CABIN AT GREAT SAND DUNES, 1940. The cabin was built in 1928 for Harold and Eva Wellington and their two children. After Frank Wellington (right) retired in 1936, he spent a lot of time at the cabin entertaining visitors like Guy Bourgain (left) from Kansas. (GRSA-736.)

Summer 1940 at the Wellington Cabin. The Bourgain family from Kansas visited the Wellington cabin. Here, Emma Bourgain (left) chats with a neighbor identified only as Ellen (right). Note Emma's dress and hairstyle—she is also in the photograph at left with her back to the viewer. (GRSA-738.)

Frank Wellington Still Digging Ditches, 1940. Even at the age of 71, Frank (top right) was still digging irrigation ditches. He was assisted by Emma Bourgain (bottom right) and her children Beulah (bottom left) and Guy (top left). (GRSA-739.)

WELLINGTON CABIN, 1964. By 1964, the cabin was in a sad state of deterioration. Frank Wellington died in 1963, and ownership passed to his son Ernest. Ernest then sold the land to the National Park Service for inclusion in Great Sand Dunes National Monument, which surrounded it. (GRSA-2145.)

SAND DUNES VIEW FROM WELLINGTON CABIN, 1964. The Wellington land was first claimed by Ernest Wellington in 1928, recorded as Township No. 27 South, Range No. 73 West, Sixth Principal Meridian. The federal government withdrew the land around the dunes from homesteading in 1930, preventing further inholdings in what became Great Sand Dunes National Monument in 1932. (GRSA-2144.)

Wellington Cabin, 2012. Snow and time continue to ravage the cabin, and the front porch has now collapsed. The National Park Service has deemed the structure not worth preserving. Leona Wellington vividly recalls collecting pinion nuts from the surrounding pine trees with her grandfather Frank in the 1950s.

Wellington Ditch Trail, May 10, 2012. The Great Sand Dunes (visible in the background) and the trail are covered by a late-spring snow. Although the Wellington cabin may someday collapse, the family name and legacy are preserved in this trail commemorating Frank Wellington's irrigation ditch.

Six

Miners around the Dunes

With the 2004 expansion of the Great Sand Dunes from a national monument to a national park, 64,000 acres of the former Baca Grant were added on the northwest. This expansion opened up land to park visitors in an area that had been heavily exploited for gold mining from the 1870s to about 1914. Hikers can now travel the dirt road from the north park boundary south toward the remains of mining camps at Duncan and Liberty.

John Duncan was born in Indiana in 1851 and, after hearing stories from men in John Fremont's expedition about of the possibility of gold in the Sangre de Cristo Mountains, he set off for the mountains in 1874. Duncan did discover gold on Milwaukee Hill, just north of Pole Creek. He often made trips east to Pueblo to take his gold ore to the smelter there. By the 1890s, Duncan had built a permanent one-room log cabin, which still stands today. Droves of people came to the area seeking their fortune in gold, and Duncan proceeded to sell lots to them, thereby founding the town of Duncan. The Duncan Post Office existed from 1892 to 1900.

The only problem was that John Duncan did not actually own the land. Duncan was located on the Baca Grant, and a US Supreme Court ruling in 1897 gave the grant all rights to the surface and minerals below the surface. Owners of the grant began evicting Duncan residents that year, and Duncan was deserted by 1900. Residents moved north to Crestone or southeast to Liberty, an appropriately named settlement just a mile away from Duncan outside the boundary line of the grant. Liberty boomed until the mines closed permanently in 1914, but the town hung on until there were so few people that the Liberty Post Office was closed in 1919.

In the late 1920s, other gold mining occurred in the Great Sand Dunes on Medano Creek, where dredges and sluices were used to process the gold-bearing sand with little success. These operations should have ceased with the creation of the national monument in 1932, but with no rangers present, they continued for a number of years.

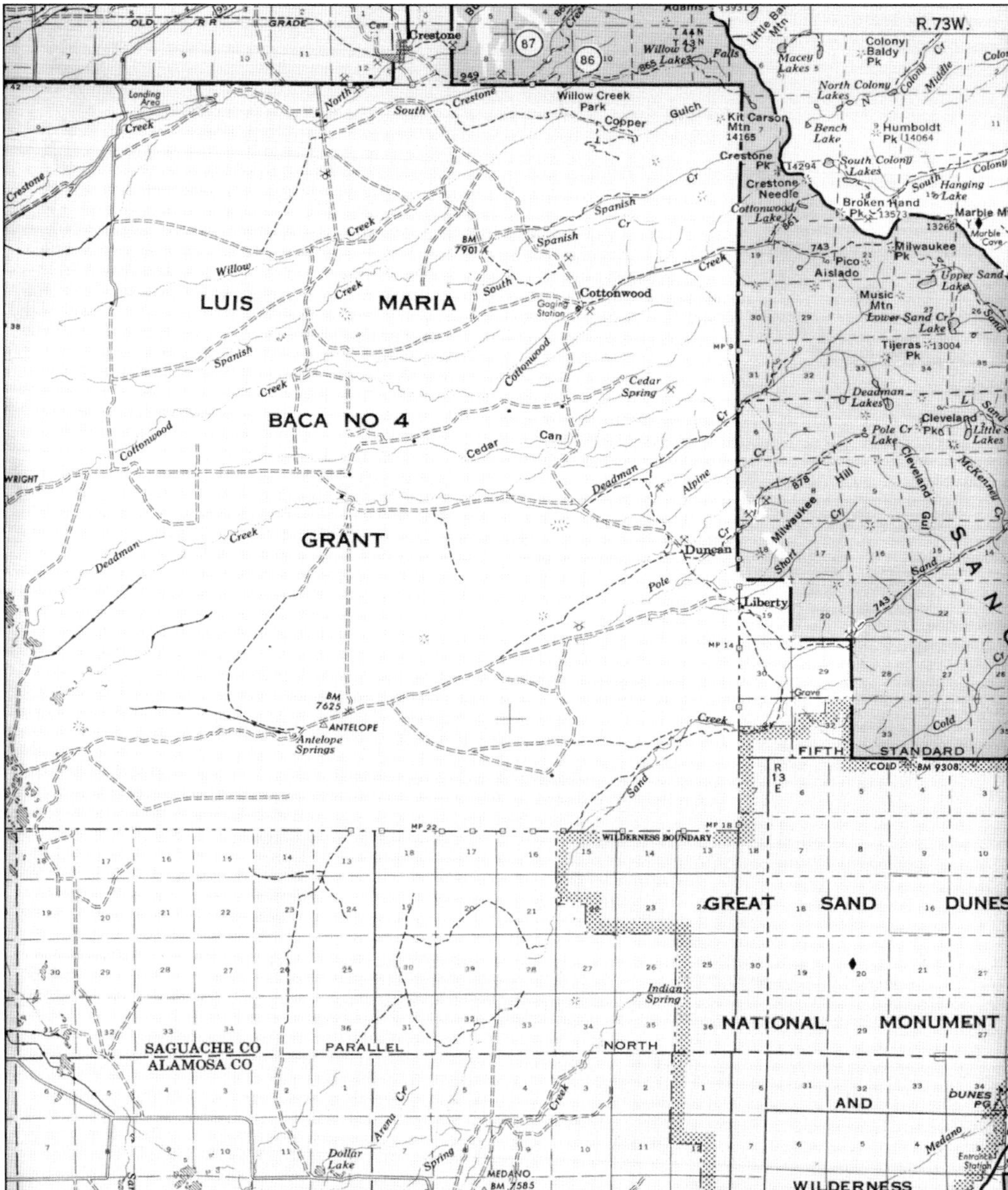

Baca Grant and Great Sand Dunes. This map from 1975 shows the relative location of the Baca Grant to Great Sand Dunes National Monument. Note how Duncan is within the Grant boundary and Liberty is just outside the boundary. Today's national park boundary extends north to the intersection of Cedar Spring Road and Duncan Road. Duncan and Liberty are just east of the new national park boundary. (US Geological Survey.)

Liberty Gate, 2012. The gate on the road to Duncan and Liberty is now open for vehicle traffic to the new trailhead parking area that was completed in 2011 and 2012. This northernmost outpost of Great Sand Dunes National Park can be reached by driving south from Crestone through the Baca Grande subdivision.

Liberty Trailhead Parking, 2012. A restroom and plenty of parking spaces are now available at the trailhead. From here, it is three and four-fifths miles of hiking on a very sandy road to Duncan with Liberty one mile farther on. The view is looking south to the Great Sand Dunes and Blanca Peak.

Great Sand Dunes and Blanca Peak, 2012. This telephoto view looks south from the Liberty Trailhead parking lot. This trail is best avoided in the hot summer season, and those who hike it should be sure to carry plenty of water.

Trail Crossing at Deadman Creek, 2012. Deadman Creek is one and four-fifths of a mile south of the Liberty Trailhead parking lot, and it is another two miles to Duncan from here. The Herard family settled near Deadman Creek in 1872 but had to move south to Medano Canyon in 1875 when they learned they were on the Baca Grant.

JOHN DUNCAN'S CABIN, 2009. Government personnel discuss the restoration of the Duncan cabin. Once the center of a thriving gold-mining community, Duncan residents were evicted by Baca Grant owners and US marshals between 1897 and 1900. All that remains are John Duncan's cabin and a log structure across the road. (GRSA.)

JOHN DUNCAN'S CABIN, 2012. In 2011 and 2012, restoration of the cabin was completed by the US Forest Service. The building, which contains several bunk beds, a stove, kitchen, table, and chairs, can be rented from the US Forest Service for overnight visits.

Milwaukee Hill at Duncan's Cabin, 2012. The highest peak in this image is Milwaukee Hill, where John Duncan discovered gold in the 1870s. The outhouse is a new addition behind the restored Duncan cabin to serve overnight guests.

Log Structure at Duncan, 2012. This structure is on the west side of the road to Liberty, while the Duncan cabin is on the east side of the road. The road serves as a boundary line with Great Sand Dunes National Park on the west, and Rio Grande National Forest on the east.

Hotel Liberty, 1907. Ruth Saunders (far left) and Julia Herard (second from left) often made the eight-mile trip on horseback from the Herard Ranch in Medano Canyon to Liberty where they would purchase supplies. With the demise of Duncan, Liberty became a key supply town for local miners and ranchers. (GRSA-5274.)

Cabin at Liberty, c. 2009. Several cabins remain at Liberty today, all on private property. Liberty had a general store with a post office (1900–1919) and a hotel, which always served one dish of wild-game meat at the evening meal. With all the miners passing through, the town was a real "hair raiser," according to one old-timer. (GRSA.)

GOLD STAMP MILL, c. 1990s. The remains of this late-1800s gold stamp mill can be found along Sand Creek in the north central portion of Great Sand Dunes National Park. Other gold-ore mills were located north of here on Pole Creek, near Duncan. (GRSA.)

GOLD DREDGE ON MEDANO CREEK, 1938. This gold dredge was part of the Volcanic Mining Company operation from the late 1920s to the early 1930s. It was located near the present-day picnic-area parking lot in Great Sand Dunes National Park. (GRSA-2152.)

HERARD-WILLIAMS FAMILY AT VOLCANIC MILL, 1930. Julia Herard Williams (seated right, in the dark outfit) was joined by her husband, John Williams (standing rear), and sons Bill and Jack (behind Julia) on this family outing to the mill. Seated to the left is Irene Tracy. (GRSA-5267.)

VOLCANIC MINING COMPANY MILL, LATE 1930s. George Opencar of Blanca established this mill to process gold, which was dredged or sluiced from the sandbars in Medano Creek. Little gold was actually found, and the operation soon fell into ruins. (GRSA.)

Water Pipeline to Volcanic Mining Company, 1929. The pipeline in the lower left of this image brought water from the mountains to the Volcanic Mining Company. This water was necessary for mining operations when Medano Creek dried up in the summer. (GRSA-2221.)

Mining Artifacts, Medano Creek, c. 2000. When Medano Creek runs low, remains of the old Volcanic Mining Company operations can be seen in the creek bed. Oil and gas drilling are new mining threats to the national park with two bores previously drilled on the Baca Grant now inside the park. Two more drill holes are proposed for the adjacent Baca National Wildlife Refuge. (GRSA.)

Seven

National Monument Formative Years

In the late 1920s and early 1930s, mining and homesteading were very real threats to the existence of the Great Sand Dunes. Residents from Alamosa to Monte Vista and as far away as Pueblo recognized the value of tourism to the dunes. As early as 1926, the Alamosa Chamber of Commerce had erected markers to direct tourists to the dunes. However, preservation of the dunes was necessary if tourists were to continue coming to the area. On June 30, 1930, Elizabeth Spencer presented a program on preserving the dunes to her PEO chapter in Monte Vista. The group formed a committee to lobby the Colorado Legislature to protect the dunes. In turn, the legislature petitioned the Colorado congressional delegation to seek protection of the dunes as a national monument.

Recognizing the growing movement to preserve the Great Sand Dunes, the federal government withdrew the dunes and the surrounding area from homesteading in 1930. The National Park Service assigned Roger Toll, its chief investigator of proposed national parks and monuments, to examine the Great Sand Dunes. Toll was also the superintendent of Yellowstone National Park and a member of the Colorado Mountain Club. Departing his winter office in Denver on February 12, 1931, Toll traveled to Alamosa by train and proceeded to inspect the Great Sand Dunes on February 13 and 14, 1931. His subsequent report to National Park Service director Horace Albright recommended that the Great Sand Dunes be preserved as a national monument. The recommendation made its way to Pres. Herbert Hoover, who signed the proclamation creating the Great Sand Dunes National Monument on March 17, 1932.

The 1930s were the era of the Great Depression, and little could be done immediately to protect the dunes or develop facilities for tourists. Late in the decade, workers from the federal economic recovery programs of the Works Progress Administration (WPA) and Civilian Conservation Corps (CCC) were used to construct rudimentary facilities, such as picnic tables, fire pits, and outhouses in Great Sand Dunes. With construction of the superintendent's headquarters and home in 1939, infrastructural development finally began in the new national monument.

Road to the Dunes, 1929. This Louis Wilhelm photograph shows the primitive two-track road to the dunes in 1929. Even though the Alamosa Chamber of Commerce posted directional signs to the dunes in 1926, automobile travel was still quite difficult on the primitive roads. (GRSA-2219.)

Road to the Dunes, 1964. Park naturalist Warren Hill took this photograph in 1964 to contrast it with Wilhelm's 1929 photograph (above). After 35 years, the only noticeable change is the road improvement. (GRSA-5614.)

Road to the Dunes, 1934. Park naturalist P.R. Franke's photograph shows the road to the dunes. Inspector Roger Toll traveled this road in February 1931 and in his report noted that "cars may be driven to within a quarter or half mile of the southeastern edge of the dune area." (GRSA.)

Roger W. Toll, c. 1930. Park inspector Toll holds a hopefully "tame" bobcat. Toll was superintendent of Yellowstone National Park from 1929 to 1936. He inspected Great Sand Dunes in 1931, favorably recommending it for national monument status. He died in a car crash in 1936 as he was returning from an inspection of Big Bend in Texas. (National Park Service.)

Jean Corlett, PEO, c. 1930. Jean Corlett was a member of the Monte Vista Chapter V PEO committee, which was formed to campaign for the designation of Great Sand Dunes as a national monument in order to save and protect it for future generations. (GRSA.)

George Corlett, c. 1930. The husband of Jean, George was a Monte Vista attorney and former Colorado lieutenant governor. He donated his time to the PEO committee to help draft a petition to the Colorado Legislature in support of Great Sand Dunes as a national monument. (GRSA.)

Myrtle Woods, PEO, c. 1930. Myrtle was also on the Monte Vista PEO committee promoting Great Sand Dunes as a national monument. PEO is a philanthropic educational organization that raises funds for scholarships to help young women attend college. (GRSA.)

PEO Letter to Colorado Senator Phipps. Having gained the support of the Colorado Legislature, the PEO committee carried on their campaign to the US Senate. Success came in 1932, when Pres. Herbert Hoover proclaimed the creation of Great Sand Dunes National Monument. (GRSA.)

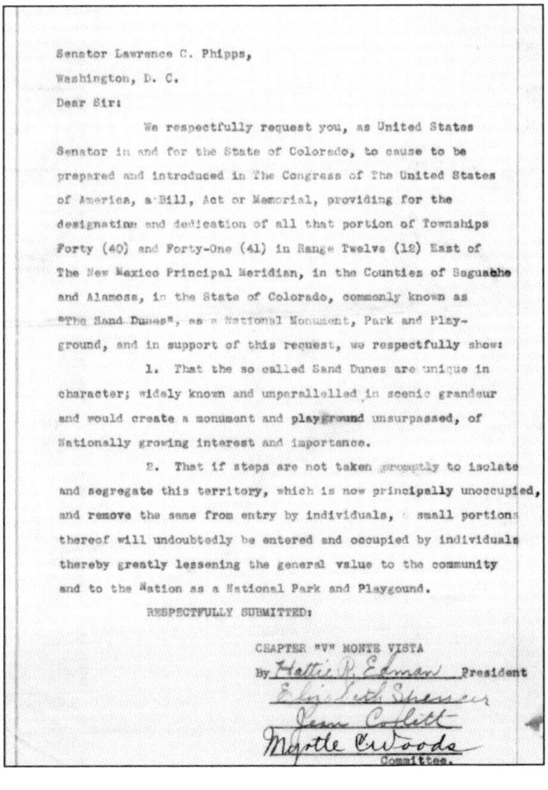

Senator Lawrence C. Phipps,

Washington, D. C.

Dear Sir:

We respectfully request you, as United States Senator in and for the State of Colorado, to cause to be prepared and introduced in The Congress of The United States of America, a Bill, Act or Memorial, providing for the designation and dedication of all that portion of Townships Forty (40) and Forty-One (41) in Range Twelve (12) East of The New Mexico Principal Meridian, in the Counties of Saguache and Alamosa, in the State of Colorado, commonly known as "The Sand Dunes", as a National Monument, Park and Playground, and in support of this request, we respectfully show:

1. That the so called Sand Dunes are unique in character; widely known and unparallelled in scenic grandeur and would create a monument and playground unsurpassed, of Nationally growing interest and importance.

2. That if steps are not taken promptly to isolate and segregate this territory, which is now principally unoccupied, and remove the same from entry by individuals, small portions thereof will undoubtedly be entered and occupied by individuals thereby greatly lessening the general value to the community and to the Nation as a National Park and Playgound.

RESPECTFULLY SUBMITTED:

CHAPTER "V" MONTE VISTA
By Hattie R. Edman President
Elizabeth Spencer
Jean Collett
Myrtle C. Woods
Committee.

Early Officials on the Dunes. Unfortunately, Great Sand Dunes has no record of the date of this photograph or the identities of these men. It was probably not Roger Toll's inspection party, which consisted only of Toll and Forest Service ranger Paul Gilbert Sr. Toll and Gilbert drove a car and then walked onto the dunes. (GRSA.)

Early Dunes Visitors. These early visitors to the Great Sand Dunes struggled through the sand of the dry Medano Creek bed to head toward the dunes. (GRSA.)

Roads to the Dunes, 1934. By 1934, graded gravel roads reached nearly to Great Sand Dunes. This view looks north on State Highway 156 (today's Highway 150) to its junction with the road from Mosca, State Highway 150 (today's County Lane 6). The Mosca road was opened in 1930. (GRSA.)

"Skiing" on the Dunes, September 1930. As part of a promotional film of the state, the Colorado Association filmed men skiing on the Great Sand Dunes. They reported that "the skis slid well on the sand for considerable distances, often attaining speeds almost as fast as on similar slopes of snow." These still photographs from the film were included in Roger Toll's report. (GRSA.)

SAND DUNES EXCURSION. Even before creation of the Great Sand Dunes National Monument in 1932, groups of people were visiting the dunes. Pictured about 1930, this Moffat School picnic group clambered up the dunes to dizzying heights. (GRSA-745.)

LINGER FAMILY PICNIC. The Linger family (owners of the Medano Ranch) enjoyed an evening cookout at Great Sand Dunes in 1935. Adults enjoyed Colorado's favorite Coors beer, especially after Prohibition ended in 1933. (GRSA.)

SUPERINTENDENT'S HOME AND PARK HEADQUARTERS, 1946. Designed by Santa Fe architect Kenneth Saunders, construction of this building began in 1939. The *Walsenburg World Independent* reported that "the building is to be made of adobe and the architecture will be the Spanish ranch house type so common in the San Luis Valley." (GRSA-2204).

PARK HEADQUARTERS AND CHECK STATION, 1946. The Colorado Historical Society noted that the superintendent's complex "was the largest project undertaken by the Works Progress Administration during its late 1930s work at Great Sand Dunes." Before this, first park employee Glen King was stationed north of the Zapata Ranch to count cars entering the new national monument. (GRSA-2205.)

SUPT. TED SOWERS AT HEADQUARTERS, 1949. From 1932 to 1946, Great Sand Dunes National Monument was administered by the superintendent of Mesa Verde National Park. Great Sand Dunes finally received its own superintendent with the appointment of Ted Sowers in 1946. Sowers served until 1950. (GRSA-2172.)

COURTYARD OF PARK SUPERINTENDENT'S HOME, 1946. The home is to the right, separated by a courtyard from the administrative check station on the left. The home was used as the superintendent's residence until 1988, when it was converted to park administration offices. (GRSA-2203.)

Porch Detail of Superintendent's Home, 1946. The home was built in the Spanish-territorial style using adobe. The windows look west to the Great Sand Dunes with the Sangre de Cristo Mountains rising behind the building. (GRSA-2202.)

Rear View of Superintendent's Home, 1944. This view of the rear of the home shows the huge expanse of the Great Sand Dunes. (GRSA-2201.)

Dirt Road to the Dunes, c. 1940s. A rather primitive road led to the dunes parking lot in the 1940s; it was not paved until 1959. To this day, this spot serves as the access point for hikers to cross Medano Creek and begin climbing the dunes. (GRSA-2292.)

Dunes Parking Lot, c. 1940s. In this image, a single car can be seen in the parking lot next to Medano Creek and the dunes. Facilities built here in 1938 by the WPA and CCC included picnic tables, fire pits, and toilets. Paved and expanded today, the parking lot can now hold hundreds of vehicles. (GRSA-2168.)

The Army Comes to the Dunes, c. 1940s. The US Army used the Great Sand Dunes as a training area for troops being sent to the desert of North Africa during World War II. Bob Linger at the Medano Ranch recalled huge convoys coming west over La Veta Pass to the dunes, and from the ranch "[they] could see this huge dust cloud" created by all the trucks on the dirt roads. (GRSA.)

Wind-Whipped Dunes, August 31, 1944. In this photograph by Natt Dodge, the dunes appear to be whipped like meringue on top of a pie. Cleveland Peak is seen at the left. (GRSA-2290.)

SHRINERS TENT ON THE DUNES, AUGUST 1947. The *Pueblo Chieftain* newspaper reported, "The Great Sand Dunes will be interwoven with the romantic and historical background of the Shriners of North America when Al Kaly Shrine temple uses the unique setting for a big ceremonial August 15 and 16." (MVHS.)

SHRINERS HEAD BACK FROM THE DUNES, AUGUST 1947. The *Pueblo Chieftain* continued their story, reporting, "A caravan of trucks will transport from Al Kaly temple in Pueblo to the Great Sand Dunes two large tents and all of the lavish costumes, trappings and equipment for the ceremonial, which will be for Shriners only."

Castle Creek Area, 1951. Supt. Glen Bean, second superintendent of Great Sand Dunes from 1950 to 1953, took this photograph near where Castle Creek enters Medano Creek. Note the vehicle in the Medano Creek bed. Driving off-road is strictly prohibited today. (GRSA-2244.)

Ghost Forest of Dead Ponderosa Pines, 1951. Superintendent Bean also took this photograph of "escape dunes," where sand has escaped the main dunefield, blowing east of Medano Creek and smothering the ponderosa pine forest. Water in Medano Creek generally helps prevent even larger areas of escape dunes from forming. (GRSA-2257.)

Dry Medano Creek Bed, November 1955. In this photograph by Natt Dodge, two visitors walk the rippled sand in the creek bed, gazing north to the dunes and a snowcapped Cleveland Peak. (GRSA-2286.)

Dry Medano Creek Bed, November 1955. As winter sets in, the park sees few visitors, as witnessed in this image (also by Natt Dodge). Up to 1955, Great Sand Dunes National Monument had fairly primitive facilities for visitors, but that situation began to change dramatically in 1956. (GRSA-2280.)

Eight

National Monument Modern Years

Visitation at Great Sand Dunes National Monument in 1958 totaled 41,000 guests, quadruple Roger Toll's 1931 estimate of 10,000. This increase was particularly amazing considering the poor condition of roads to the dunes and the virtual lack of any visitor facilities (other than a few picnic tables). There was no visitor center, no campground, and no amphitheater. Nationwide, the national parks were still operating with dilapidated facilities designed for 17 million visitors in 1940 but were being inundated with 54 million visitors in 1954. Staffing levels from 1940 had not been increased either.

Viewing this situation in 1951, the new director of the National Park Service, Conrad L. Wirth, decided to take a bold step. He saw the advantage of placing the entire national parks want list together in one funding package, rather than going at it piecemeal. He developed a 10-year program, which would begin in 1956 and endeavor to bring every park up to standard by 1966. The program was called Mission 66 in celebration of the 50th anniversary of the National Park Service in 1966, which would also be the year of the building program's completion. Its budgeted cost was $800 million, but expenses came to $1 billion by the time it was completed.

For Great Sand Dunes, Mission 66 finally brought about the facilities needed by visitors. The entrance road was paved in 1959, and construction of the Visitor Center began in 1961. A maintenance building was also constructed in 1961, followed by Pinyon Flats Campground in 1963 and employee housing in 1964. Finally, in 1966, an amphitheater with seating for 500 people was constructed. The Mission 66 projects were so successful for Great Sand Dunes that visitation again more than quadrupled with 178,000 visitors arriving in 1968.

Great Sand Dunes National Monument was born in the Great Depression, and visitor infrastructure was basically neglected until the Mission 66 program began. Then, with the escalation of the Vietnam War in 1966, funding for the national park system was again curtailed. There would not be another major investment in the dunes until the expansion of the Visitor Center in 1997.

Entrance Station, June 1958. Great Sand Dunes superintendent Harold Schaafsma (left) greets National Parks Service director Conrad Wirth at the entrance station. Wirth was the creator of the Mission 66 national parks improvement program. (GRSA-2176.)

Entrance Road. One of the first projects of Mission 66 in Great Sand Dunes was the paving of the entrance road in 1959. To the right in this image, a snowcapped Mount Herard rises majestically above the dunes. (GRSA.)

VISITOR CENTER CONSTRUCTION, AUGUST 1961. The sweeping curve of the Visitor Center patio is seen here under construction in 1961. The view is looking south toward the San Luis Valley. (GRSA-2191.)

COMPLETED VISITOR CENTER PATIO, AUGUST, 1963. Superintendent Schaafsma (right) chats with three visitors on the patio. (GRSA-2173.)

VISITOR CENTER CONSTRUCTION, OCTOBER 1961. The Visitor Center is well under way in this view looking north to the Sangre de Cristo Mountains. (GRSA-2195.)

VISITOR CENTER ENTRANCE CONSTRUCTION, OCTOBER 1961. This westward view shows the front entrance to the building. The Great Sand Dunes would be directly visible from the patio on the opposite side of the building. (GRSA-2196.)

VISITOR CENTER, c. 1970. Built with basic concrete-block construction, the Visitor Center reflected Mission 66 architecture, quite different from the Spanish-territorial flavor of the superintendent's residence. (GRSA.)

VISITOR CENTER, AUTUMN 1970. Autumn changes the leaves on the cottonwood trees to a brilliant gold color, both on the mountain slopes (foreground) and along the dry Medano Creek bed (middle ground). (GRSA.)

Maintenance Building Under Construction, August 1961. Mission 66 funds also provided for the first maintenance building at Great Sand Dunes. Here, vehicles and equipment would be serviced and repaired. (GRSA-2212.)

Maintenance Building, June 2012. The only change since 1961 appears to be the addition of one more garage stall at the left of the building.

Employee Housing, November 1964. Mission 66 funds allowed for the construction of employee housing east of the maintenance building. This is building No. 14, a three-unit apartment structure. (GRSA-2177.)

Building No. 14, Rear View, November 1964. In these apartments nestled on the flank of the Sangre de Cristo Mountains, employees were surrounded by mountains and piñon pine trees. (GRSA-2178.)

Residence No. 8, January 1966. This single-family residence served as home for the caretaker of Great Sand Dunes National Monument. At the time of this photograph, it housed the Ben King family. (GRSA-2179.)

Caretaker Ben King, May 14, 1965. One of caretaker Ben King's more exotic duties was examining the bodies of these two dead bobcats that were killed after climbing a power pole south of the Visitor Center. According to notes accompanying the photograph, the bobcats shorted out the wires, causing a power failure at 4:10 a.m. (GRSA-2619.)

Picnic Area and Dunes Parking Lot, July 4, 1971. Mission 66 funds allowed for the expansion and pavement of the dunes parking lot as well as the addition of picnic shelters (seen here, where a large crowd is enjoying Fourth of July festivities). (GRSA-2161.)

Walkway to the Dunes, 1984. This boardwalk led from the dunes parking lot to Medano Creek and the dunes. Today, this walkway consists of nonslip rubber mats. The sign reads "Driving Off Roadway Prohibited—No Parking On Dunes." (MVHS.)

New Road to Pinyon Flats Campground, October 1964. The road from the dunes parking lot to the new campground was not yet paved when this photograph was taken. Mission 66 funds provided for the construction of the campground in 1963. (GRSA-2297.)

Camper Trailer Leaving the Campground, c. 1970. The campground proved extremely popular with visitors, and in 1965, it registered 27,000 camper visits only two years after opening. (GRSA-5453.)

Pinyon Flats Campground, August 1963. Newly completed, the campground saw trailers packed together side by side in 1963. The spot has always been first come, first served; for those not finding a site, space is available at the Oasis campground, just south of the park boundary. (GRSA-2165.)

Pinyon Flats Campground, July 1987. Heavy crowding (as seen in the previous photograph) prompted the National Park Service to post a regulation limiting each site to a single vehicle. (GRSA-5629.)

Campfire Program, Summer 1963. Prior to the construction of the permanent amphitheater in 1966, this makeshift venue near the dunes provided log benches for visitors with a plywood screen for slide shows. Supt. Harold Schaafsma is shown standing in the photograph. (GRSA-2174.)

Amphitheater Constructed in 1966. The Hawkinson-Olson Construction Company of Farmington, New Mexico, was low bidder on the project at $35,000. The *Rocky Mountain News* reported that "the outdoor theater will seat 500 persons, and will be equipped with projection equipment as well as a stereophonic sound system for the popular nightly programs presented during the summer season by park naturalists." (GRSA.)

Amphitheater, c. 1980s. A puppet show entertained young visitors on this summer day with the Great Sand Dunes looming in the background. (GRSA.)

Amphitheater, June 2012. The amphitheater seating remains unchanged, but the first amphitheater building burned down in the wildfire of 2000. The stage area was then reconstructed into a Spanish-adobe style to match the new style for the Visitor Center.

Pond in Dunes, June 1958. The vast majority of Great Sand Dunes is wilderness, unaffected by Mission 66 construction. Here, a small pond formed between dune crests. In the background are the Crestone Peaks (left) and Cleveland Peak (center.) (GRSA-2249.)

Lone Hiker on the Dunes, c. 1960. Footprints in the sand ripples lead to a solitary hiker. There are no trails within the dunefield, so hikers must climb to the top of a dune to get their bearings. (GRSA-5606.)

Sunflowers Bloom on the Sand Sheet, August 1965. Southwest of the dunefield, there was enough moisture in the sand sheet to support this group of sunflowers in the summer of 1965. Cleveland Peak is in the center background, and Mount Herard is seen to the right. (GRSA-2270.)

Solitary Sunflower on the Dunes, 1961. During normal moisture years, sunflowers are common on the dunes in mid-August. (GRSA-5595.)

College Students Surfing Down Dune, May 1965. Since at least the 1930s, adventurous visitors have been skiing, surfing, or snowboarding down the dunes. (GRSA-2620.)

Hikers on Medano Pass Primitive Road, July 1987. For those not wishing to "ski" down the dunes, more conventional hiking trails and roads exist. This road may be driven by four-wheel-drive vehicles to the remains of the Herard homestead in Medano Canyon and then on to Medano Pass. (GRSA-5629.)

BACKCOUNTRY BOUNDARY, DECEMBER 1970. If the snow is not too deep, driving the Medano Pass Primitive Road over the sand is actually easier in winter because the sand is compacted under the snow, and vehicles do not sink in as they do in summer. (GRSA.)

FOUR-WHEEL-DRIVE TOURS, C. 1970S. The Sand Dunes Oasis, just south of the monument boundary, offered four-wheel-drive tours into Great Sand Dunes National Monument during the 1970s. Specially built long truck beds could carry about a dozen visitors to the dunes. (GRSA.)

Four-Wheel-Drive Trucks on the Dunes, 1973. Before stricter regulations were imposed by the National Park Service, these vehicles were allowed to drive off-road in the Medano Creek bed, dropping off visitors at the base of the dunes.

Driving in Medano Creek, August 1975. These visitors were having a great time splashing along in Medano Creek. By 1984, vehicles were no longer allowed to drive off-road in the national monument. (GRSA.)

Helicopter Unloads Troops at the Dunes, 1987. This helicopter dropped off troops (probably from Fort Carson in Colorado Springs) for maneuvers in the Great Sand Dunes. The precedent for troop maneuvers at the dunes had been set in the 1940s. (GRSA-5455.)

Maneuvers at the Dunes, 1987. Troops line up for the three-mile hike to the campground, where they will be based during maneuvers. Park superintendent Robert Reyes assists with traffic control on the busy main road into the park. (GRSA-5455.)

Medano Road Nature Walk, July 1987. Ranger Kris Medina is pictured leading the morning nature walk, pointing out grasses, shrubs, trees, and other features of the ecological system to park visitors. (GRSA-5629.)

Cooling Off in Medano Creek, July 1987. Jason Butler cools off after climbing the dunes in the Castle Creek area on a hot July afternoon. Sand temperatures on the dunes can easily reach 140 degrees Fahrenheit on summer afternoons.

Nine

National Park Ecosystem Preserved

Great Sand Dunes National Monument had a watershed year, both literally and figuratively, in 1991. Since 1986, American Water Development, Inc. (AWDI), owner of the Baca Ranch just northwest of the dunes, had threatened to sell 200,000 acre-feet of groundwater annually from the Baca Ranch to Colorado's Front Range cities. In 1991, a federal judge determined that AWDI did not have senior rights to the water. AWDI appealed to the US Supreme Court, which, in 1994, upheld the previous ruling. A coalition of farmers, ranchers, environmentalists, and the National Park Service personnel breathed a sigh of relief when the Supreme Court ruling came down.

Since the development of the water exportation threat in 1986, geologists had been able to determine the extreme effects that the loss of this much groundwater would have on San Luis Valley ranchers and on Great Sand Dunes. Lowering the water table would have caused a loss of creek flow around the dunes, changing the dunefield's erosion and deposition processes. The effects would also have been detrimental to San Luis Valley farmers and ranchers, whose livelihoods depended on groundwater pumped to irrigate their fields.

Having survived one hurdle, the coalition met a second one when, in 1995, yet another new owner of the Baca Ranch proposed to sell 150,000 acre-feet of groundwater. Although this threat came to nothing, the coalition had learned its lesson and began earnestly planning to protect Great Sand Dunes and the San Luis Valley. The Nature Conservancy was enlisted to purchase the large ranches around Great Sand Dunes with the intent of protecting the groundwater. In 1999, the Nature Conservancy purchased the combined Medano-Zapata Ranches, and an agreement was reached to eventually purchase the Baca Ranch. In 2000, Congress passed the Great Sand Dunes National Park and Preserve Act, which would create a new national park when the purchase of the Baca Ranch was completed.

In 2004, the Nature Conservancy finalized purchase of the Baca Ranch, land was transferred to the National Park Service, and Great Sand Dunes National Park & Preserve officially came into existence on September 13 of that year.

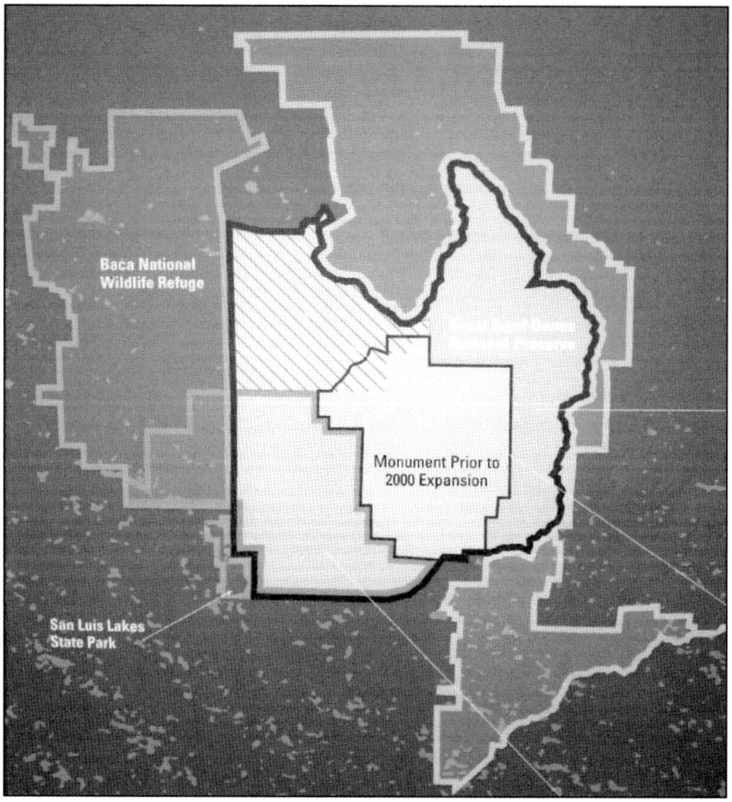

Piecing Together a National Park, 2004. The national park and preserve is outlined by the dark black line on the map. The mountain watershed on the east was protected by the new Great Sand Dunes National Preserve formed from Rio Grande National Forest. Groundwater supplies were protected on the northwest by adding a portion of the Baca Ranch (diagonal lines) and on the southwest by adding the Medano Ranch. (GRSA.)

National Park Entrance, May 10, 2012. The park entrance is pictured on a snowy spring day. The Great Sand Dunes ecosystem is preserved for now, and only time will tell what other threats the future might bring.

SIGN AT THE ZAPATA RANCH. The Nature Conservancy purchased the combined Medano-Zapata Ranch in 1999. The Medano Ranch (northern) portion has now been included inside the boundary of Great Sand Dunes National Park, while the Zapata Ranch (southern) portion is outside the park.

VIEW EAST FROM MEDANO RANCH, 2012. Now inside the national park, the former Medano Ranch offers this spectacular view of the Great Sand Dunes, the Crestone Peaks (left), and Cleveland Peak (right).

SAN LUIS LAKE STATE PARK, 2012. The management mosaic preserving the Great Sand Dunes ecosystem includes the US Forest Service, National Park Service, Nature Conservancy, and Colorado State Parks. This state park preserves the *sabkha* land adjacent to the southwest corner of the national park.

SAN LUIS LAKE, APRIL 28, 1925. This O.T. Davis photograph shows fishermen at the lake, the Great Sand Dunes to the northeast, and the Sangre de Cristo Mountains. The lake is part of the *sabkha* area, where underground water rises to the surface to form small lakes and ponds. (MVHS.)

BACA NATIONAL WILDLIFE REFUGE, 2012. The Nature Conservancy's purchase of the Baca Ranch was split into three parcels—the northeast mountain-peak area went to Rio Grande National Forest; the southeast sand sheet and dunes went to Great Sand Dunes National Park; and the western half became Baca National Wildlife Refuge, which is not yet open to the public.

MOUNT HERARD TOWERS OVER MEDANO LAKE, AUGUST 2005. The mountain watershed where Sand Creek and Medano Creek originate is now protected in Great Sand Dunes National Preserve, administered by the national park. Medano Lake can be reached by hikers on a three-mile trail from the Medano Pass Primitive Road.

Oil Well near Mosca, September 1911. This O.T. Davis photograph illustrates the oil drilling that has occurred for over 100 years near the Great Sand Dunes. Two plugged oil bores from the former Baca Ranch are now within the boundary of Great Sand Dunes National Park, and two more oil bores are proposed for Baca National Wildlife Refuge. (MVHS.)

Baca Grande Subdivision, 2012. Just south of Crestone, this housing subdivision was created in 1971 from the northeast corner of the Baca Ranch by the ranch owner. It was envisioned as a retirement community with 10,000 lots laid out on 14,000 acres. Such a large encroachment on the natural environment helped spur creation of Great Sand Dunes National Park.

DUNEFIELD AND ESCAPE DUNE, NOVEMBER 1955. Medano Creek cuts through here, keeping the large dunefield in check. Water harvesting schemes of the 1980s threatened to diminish Sand Creek and Medano Creek, disrupting the equilibrium of the ecosystem now preserved in the national park. (GRSA-2278.)

SOLAR ENERGY IN SAN LUIS VALLEY, 2012. Abundant sunshine in the San Luis Valley prompted creation of this solar-collection field near Mosca. While not an immediate threat to Great Sand Dunes, proposed power lines from here could potentially mar nearby scenic corridors.

PARK HEADQUARTERS, MAY 10, 2012. Snow lingers on the former park superintendent's home, which was converted to park offices in 1988. Comparison with earlier photographs shows complete preservation of the original complex.

PARK HEADQUARTERS COURTYARD, MAY 10, 2012. A 1997 park photograph shows the exterior of the complex painted white. Restoration of the complex in 2000 and 2001 brought back the original adobe-brown color now seen on the walls.

Visitor Center, c. 1998. Constructed in 1961, the Visitor Center was expanded and remodeled into this adobe structure in 1997. Soaring arches and columns, reminiscent of the Spanish-mission style, transformed the old concrete boxlike building to more closely match the architectural style of park headquarters. (GRSA.)

Planned Visitor Center Expansion, 2004. With national park status on the horizon, the Visitor Center was expanded once again to add the wing depicted on the right in this architectural rendering. The new Great Sand Dunes National Park would soon see visitation increase to almost 300,000 annually. (GRSA.)

Visitor Center Expansion, February 2004. This east wing of the Visitor Center was added in 2004, continuing the use of the contemporary Spanish style developed for the Visitor Center by Colorado Springs architect Morey Bean. (GRSA.)

Visitor Center Observation Deck. The former patio area has been transformed into this beautiful observation deck, complete with telescopes to view the Great Sand Dunes. (GRSA.)

Temporary Bookstore, 2004. With the official Visitor Center closed for expansion, a temporary visitor center and bookstore operated for two years in a double-wide trailer stationed in the dunes parking lot. (GRSA.)

New Park Superintendent Lisa Carrico, March 2012. Lisa Carrico, the first female superintendent of Great Sand Dunes, grew up in the Great Sand Dunes superintendent's home as the daughter of James Carrico, who held the position from 1969 to 1975. Lisa attended high school in Mosca. Her office is now located in what used to be the living room of their family home. (GRSA.)

BACKCOUNTRY NATIONAL PARK BOUNDARY, JULY 2012. This location on the Medano Pass Primitive Road now marks the boundary between the national park (beyond the sign) and the national preserve.

RAIN SHOWER MOVES IN, JULY 2012. A late-afternoon rain shower sweeps across the San Luis Valley from west to east, heading for the Great Sand Dunes. The new national park preserves the important water resources of the entire ecosystem surrounding the dunes.

Bibliography

Bean, Luther. *Land of the Blue Sky People*. Alamosa, CO: O & V Printing, 1962.

Carter, C. Joe. "Cultural History of the Great Sand Dunes." *San Luis Valley Historian*, Vol. 22, No. 3 (1990): 6–17.

Crockett, Dorothy, and Becky Frazier. "Great Sand Dunes Loom Large in P.E.O." *The P.E.O. Record*, March–April 2012: 12–15.

Everhart, William C. *The National Park Service*. New York, NY: Praeger Publishers, 1972.

Hall, Elizabeth A. *Sand Stories: Recollections of Life Around the Great Sand Dunes*. Alamosa, CO: Friends of the Dunes, 2004.

Harlan, George. *Postmarks and Places*. Monte Vista, CO: Adobe Village Press, 2002.

Harlan, Noel. "Broken Dreams: The History of Duncan Mining Camp." *San Luis Valley Historian*, Vol. 42, No. 3 (2000): 5– 21.

Jones, Cuvier. "The Herard Family." *San Luis Valley Historian*, Vol. 11, No. 1 (1979): 7–11.

Kania, Alan J., ed. "The Great Sand Dunes: Colorado History from Early Day News-papers." *Colorado Prospector*, Special Edition (1988): 1–24.

McAlpin, James. *Crestone: Gateway to the Higher Realms*. Crestone, CO: Crestone Science Center, Inc., 2011.

Rozinski, Bob, Wendy Shattil, and Audrey DeLella Benedict. *Valley of the Dunes: Great Sand Dunes National Park and Preserve*. Golden, CO: Fulcrum Publishing, 2005.

Simmons, Virginia McConnell. *The San Luis Valley: Land of the Six-Armed Cross*. Boulder, CO: Pruett Publishing, 1979.

Toll, Roger W. *Report on Great Sand Dunes National Monument*. Washington, DC: Department of the Interior, National Park Service, 1931.

Trimble, Stephen. *Great Sand Dunes: The Shape of the Wind*. Tucson, AZ: Western National Parks Association, 2007.

Winger, Charlie and Diane. *The Essential Guide to Great Sand Dunes National Park and Preserve*. Golden, CO: Colorado Mountain Club Press, 2003.

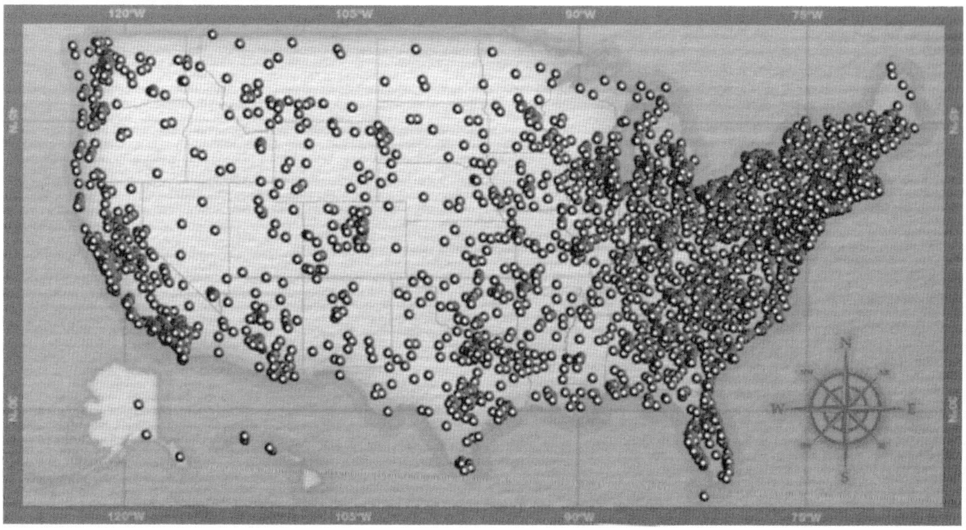